THE NEW EXPATRIATES

- THE NEW EXPATRIATES -
Managing Human Resources Abroad

Rosalie L. Tung

Ballinger Publishing Company
Cambridge, Massachusetts
A Subsidiary of Harper & Row, Publishers, Inc.

International Standard Book Number: 0-88730-133-9

Library of Congress Catalog Card Number: 87-17835

Printed in the United States of America

Library of Congress Cataloging-in-Publication Data

Tung, Rosalie L. (Rosalie Lam), 1948-
    The new expatriates: managing human resources abroad / by Rosalie L. Tung.
        p. cm.
    Bibliography: p.
    Includes index.
    ISBN 0-88730-133-9
    1. International business enterprises—Personnel management.
    2. International business enterprises—Case studies. I. Title.
HF5549.T82 1987
658.3'1—dc19   87-17835
                                                                CIP

Dedicated to the memory of
Richard N. Farmer, an inspiration
to a generation of
international business scholars

CONTENTS

LIST OF FIGURES AND TABLES

PREFACE AND ACKNOWLEDGMENTS

This book marks the third phase of my study on selection and training procedures for expatriate assignments among a sample of U.S., European, and Japanese multinationals. In an earlier study (Tung 1982) that presented the findings of a questionnaire survey comparing expatriation practices among U.S., European, and Japanese multinationals, I found that European and Japanese multinationals consistently outperformed their U.S. counterparts by a wide margin. Although some U.S. multinationals experienced failure rates as high as 30 percent (i.e., 30 percent of the people sent overseas are dismissed or recalled home because they cannot perform effectively in a foreign environment), the failure rates among the European and Japanese multinationals were under 15 percent. In fact, the majority of European and Japanese multinationals had recall rates of below 5 percent. To gain a deeper understanding of the reasons for the lower rate of expatriate failure among the European and Japanese multinationals, I embarked on in-depth case studies of human resource management practices at a sample of European and Japanese firms. The case studies of eighteen Japanese multinationals were contained in my 1984 book, *Key to Japan's Economic Strength: Human Power*.

This present volume compares and contrasts the selection and training procedures for expatriate assignments among a sample of U.S. and European multinationals, analyzes the reasons for the European multinationals' success, and shows how U.S. multinationals can learn from their European counterparts. The findings of the earlier study on Japanese multinationals (Tung 1984a) are used for comparative purposes, where relevant. Specifically, the book identifies and examines (1) the criteria used by both U.S. and European multinationals in selecting candidates for overseas assignments; (2) the kinds of training programs sponsored by U.S. and European multinationals to prepare candidates for managing, working, and living in a foreign country; (3) the failure rates of U.S. and

European multinationals; and (4) the factors responsible for the expatriate's inability to perform successfully in a foreign environment. Case studies of selected European multinationals describe and analyze the criteria they use in selecting candidates for overseas assignments; the training programs that prepare these employees for living and working in a foreign country; and methods of repatriation, an issue of particular concern to U.S. expatriates.

The case studies are based on interviews with executives in the international divisions and those in charge of training and development programs in the respective companies. The seventeen European multinationals included represent a diverse range of industries in several countries, namely, the United Kingdom, Italy, Switzerland, and the Federal Republic of Germany. Because French multinationals were inaccessible to this study, I refer the reader to a 1985 survey taken by Christophe Misrachi of Inter Cultural Management Associates, a consulting firm in Paris, France. His study summarizes the findings of nineteen French companies from ten different industries. In general, the policies and practices at these French multinationals —including the increasing emphasis placed on international experience and the high cost of expatriation—resemble those of their West European counterparts. The selection criteria, training programs, remuneration policies, and reasons for failure abroad are also similar to those of the West European firms in my study.

The findings of this volume are important to both practitioners and academicians. By learning how successful European multinationals handle expatriate assignments, practitioners will be better equipped to restructure their own existing programs. Such informed restructuring will improve not only the rate of success of future assignments but also the overall performance of the overseas subsidiaries, which would then be staffed by individuals properly trained to live and work in a foreign environment.

A comparative analysis of the selection and training procedures of expatriate assignments of U.S. and European multinationals also has implications for theory and research in the field of international management. The results will increase our understanding of the relationships between antecedent (in this case, selection criteria and training programs) and outcome variables (the success or failure of expatriate assignments) and other extraneous factors. This knowledge will contribute to the development of more appropriate and comprehensive selection procedures and training programs, which in turn will increase the efficiency and effectiveness of expatriate assignments.

I thank all those who have given their time willingly and generously to this project. Respondents to the questionnaire surveys were not required to disclose the name of their organizations, thus I cannot cite them here by name.

I am particularly grateful to those who gave their time unsparingly during the interviews to provide a comprehensive picture of their companies' human resource development programs. Specifically, I thank the following individuals: Patrick Lloyd, Center for International Briefing, Farnham Castle; Allan Hall, Center for International Briefing, Farnham Castle; Peter Rogers, Imperial Chemical Industries, P.L.C.; David Wootton, Imperial Chemical Industries, P.L.C.; David J. Hurst, National Westminster Bank, P.L.C.; Kay Pierce, National Westminster Bank, P.L.C.; Roger J. Austin, the British Petroleum Co., P.L.C.; A.J.P. Vineall, Unilever, P.L.C.; Vittorio Tesio, Fiat; Alberto Pichi, Ing. C. Olivetti & C., S.p.a.; Franco Mai, Ing. C. Olivetti & C., S.p.a.; Vincenzo Pedriali, Ing. C. Olivetti & C., S.p.a.; Michael Rowley, Ing. C. Olivetti & C., S.p.a.; Cesare Vaciago, Montedison; A. Respligi, Montedison; A.S. Scarpallegia, Montedison; Ezio Cullino, Instituto Bancario San Paolo; Luigi Capuano, Instituto Bancario San Paolo; Arnold Minder, Schhweizerischer Bankverein (Swiss Bank Corporation); Guido Kurath, Schhweizerischer Bankverein; Hans Kilchenmann, Sandoz AG; Louis Eberle, Sandoz AG; Hans Beat Gamper, Brown Boveri & Cie; Guido Richterich, F. Hoffman – La Roche & Co., Ltd.; Klaus Kramer, Siemens AG; Werner Eichenlaub, Siemens AG; and Raimund Gmeiner, Siemens AG. I also thank those executives who took part in the study but who cannot be cited here by name because they have chosen to disguise the identity of their companies.

Last, but not least, I would like to thank my husband, Byron, and daughter, Michele, for their understanding and moral support throughout the entire project. The completion of this book has kept me busy on countless evenings and weekends.

1 HUMAN RESOURCE MANAGEMENT
Key to Success in International Business Operations

In their book, *In Search of Excellence* (1982), Peters and Waterman contend that a common denominator underlying the best-run companies in the United States is the emphasis those firms place on human resource management. This is no startling revelation in itself. About thirty years ago, Peter Drucker stated in his seminal work, *The Practice of Management* (1954), that the function of management is to combine human power, capital, and technology to attain a desired level of performance in the organization. In practice, however, U.S. companies generally have emphasized the management of capital and technology, often relegating human resource development to a secondary position in their overall corporate strategic planning. Consequently, Waterman and Peters' thesis, which refocuses attention on human resource development (a soft S in the McKinsey 7-S framework) is both apt and significant at a time when U.S. firms are searching for ways to regain their international competitiveness.

It is my contention that human resource planning is pivotal to the successful operation of a multinational corporation (MNC) because technology, capital, and know-how could not be effectively and efficiently utilized nor transferred from corporate headquarters to the various worldwide subsidiaries without using human power. Any attempt at economic restructuring, industrial revitalization, or industrial targeting is

Portions of this chapter appeared in R.L. Tung, "Selection and Training of Personnel for Overseas Assignments," *Columbia Journal of World Business* (Spring 1981): 68–78, reprinted with permission; and R.L. Tung, "Selection and Training Procedures of U.S., European and Japanese Multinationals". Copyright © 1982 by the Regents of the University of California. Condensed from the *California Management Review*, Vol. 25, No. 1. By permission of The Regents.

destined to fail if adequate attention is not given to the planning, management, and deployment of human resources required in these efforts. There are many stories of how blundering American expatriates lose substantial portions of their existing or potential market shares to foreign competitors in the international marketplace for this very reason.

Consider the example of ABC Corporation, the disguised name of a major U.S. food manufacturer. ABC was seeking someone from its corporate staff to head the marketing division in Japan. Mr. X was selected because he was clearly one of the company's brightest young talents and he had demonstrated superior marketing skills in the home office. The company did not assess his ability to relate to and work with the Japanese, simply assuming that a good manager in the United States would also be a good manager abroad. Prior to his assignment, ABC gave Mr. X some literature pertaining to the geography, climate, banking institutions, and educational institutions in Japan and asked him to share this material with his family. Mr. X's assignment to Japan was to last for 18 months. In the initial six months, he was unable to devote much time to the company's activities because he and his family were preoccupied with adapting to their new environment. Similarly, in the last six months, Mr. X was busy thinking about some changes at the home office. He heard that Mr. Y, a peer and rival, had just been promoted to the position to which both men had aspired and that Mr. X had been transferred to another ABC branch. What must he do to reenter the race for advancement in the corporate organizational hierarchy? While he was strategizing, his wife was hounding him on matters related to their relocation to the West Coast such as whether to sell or lease their home in the Midwest. The result: In the course of Mr. X's 18-month assignment to Japan, ABC corporation lost 98 percent of its existing market share to a major European competitor.

Mr. X's experience does not appear to be unique. A questionnaire survey of expatriate assignments in 80 U.S. multinationals showed that more than half of the companies had failure rates of 10 to 20 percent, and some 7 percent of the respondent firms had recall rates of 30 percent (Tung 1982). In this survey, "failure" was defined as the inability of an expatriate to perform effectively in a foreign country , resulting in his being fired or recalled home. These statistics are consistent with the findings of other researchers (Adams and Kobayashi 1969; Henry 1965; Seward 1975), which showed that 30 percent or more of overseas assignments in U.S. multinationals had been mistakes. Such failures are costly to any company in time, money, and human resources. An inability to operate effectively abroad may cause a company's foreign operation to stagnate and, worse, lose its market share to competitors. Besides lost opportunities and revenues for the company, these failures often constitute heavy blows to the expatriates' self-esteem. As in the case of Mr. X, many employees who were sent abroad had been star performers with excellent records in the home office prior to their overseas assignment. Even if they are accepted back into corporate headquarters, it may take some time before they are able to regain confidence in their abilities. For all of these reasons, multinational corporations should devote more attention to human resource planning and development.

This chapter presents the results of a research survey comparing the human resource management programs for expatriate assignments among a sample of U.S., European, and Japanese multinationals. In general, it appears that the European and Japanese MNCs send abroad individuals who are more adept at living and working in a foreign environment. It is often posited that the international competitiveness of U.S. multinationals may be weakening because of the narrowing technological gap between the United States, Europe, and Japan. Perhaps a more significant reason is the fact that since European and Japanese multinationals traditionally place heavier emphasis on international markets, they devote considerably more attention to selection and training of people for overseas assignments, which in turn translates into more effective performance abroad. Conversely, because of the large size of their domestic market, U.S. corporations often relegate international sales to a secondary position in their overall corporate pictures. This attitude is often reflected in the assumption that what sells in Peoria will also have a ready market abroad. It is also manifested in staffing policies which assume that an effective manager in the United States will perform well in a foreign environment. As the story of Mr. X showed, however, this strategy does not always work.

QUESTIONNAIRE SURVEY FINDINGS

A questionnaire (see Appendix) was developed for studying the following characteristics:

1. The extent to which affiliate operations of U.S., European, and Japanese MNCs in various regions of the world are staffed by parent-country nationals (citizens of the home country of the multinational), host-country nationals (citizens of the country of foreign

operation), and third-country nationals (neither citizens of the home country of the MNC nor of the country in which the foreign operation is located);

2. The criteria used for selecting personnel to fill positions in various categories of overseas job assignments;

3. The procedures undertaken to determine a candidate's suitability for the foreign position;

4. The types of training programs used to prepare candidates in each of the job categories for overseas work; and

5. The success rate and the reasons for success.

This questionnaire was pretested with a sample of 12 U.S. personnel administrators of MNCs. As a result of the pilot study, certain terminologies and items in the questionnaire were revised to improve readability and to facilitate responses.

The questionnaire was translated from English to German, French, Spanish, Italian, Dutch, and Japanese by bilingual researchers thoroughly fluent in the respective languages. The translated questionnaires were then retranslated into English by other bilingual researchers. Comparison of the original English questionnaire against the retranslated version facilitated the identification and modification of problem phrases and terminologies.

The English-language questionnaires were sent to a sample of 300 of the largest U.S. multinationals listed in Angel's *Directory of American Firms Operating Abroad*; 105 questionnaires were returned, of which 80 were usable. Questionnaires in the respective European languages were sent to 246 West European MNCs located in Belgium, the United Kingdom, the Federal Republic of Germany, Sweden, the Netherlands, Norway, Switzerland, Denmark, France, Italy, and Spain. These companies were identified in Fortune's *Directory of the 500 Largest Industrial Companies Abroad*. None of the questionnaires sent to Denmark, France, Italy, or Spain were returned. Of the remaining 196 questionnaires sent to the other European nations, 29 usable questionnaires were returned. The Japanese-language questionnaires were sent to a sample of 110 of the largest Japanese MNCs listed in Fortune's *Directory of the 500 Largest Industrial Companies Abroad*; 35 usable ones were returned. The questionnaires for all three samples were completed by the vice president of foreign operations, or a person of some similar designation, of each of the firms.

Table 1-1. Percentage of Firms in Various Parts of the World.

	Western Europe	Canada	Middle/ Near East	Eastern Europe	Latin/ South America	Far East	Africa	United States
U.S. MNCs	95	86	66	19	91	88	71	NR
West European MNCs	100	62	48	7	66	72	69	79
Japanese MNCs	62	39	29	0	86	81	29	57

NR = Not relevant

Locations of overseas affiliates were categorized into eight regions: Western Europe, Canada, Eastern Europe, Middle and Near East, Latin and South America, Far East, Africa, and the United States. Respondents were asked to identify the regions in which they had affiliate operations. Table 1-1 presents a breakdown of the percentage of firms that had affiliate operations in each of these eight regions. As compared to the U.S. and West European samples, few or none of the Japanese MNCs had affiliate operations in the Middle and Near East, Eastern Europe, or Africa. This may reflect the stage of development of Japanese MNCs: multinationals are still a fairly recent phenomenon on the Japanese industrial scene.

ANALYSIS OF FINDINGS

Staffing Policies

Respondents were asked to identify whether management personnel at three levels (senior, middle, and lower) in each of the eight regions were primarily parent-country, host-country, or third-country nationals. Table 1-2 presents a breakdown of the responses for U.S., West European, and Japanese multinationals. Frequency distributions in the table show that for the U.S. and European samples, host-country nationals were used to a much greater extent at all levels of management in developed regions of the world as compared to the less-developed regions. This is logical, as

Table 1–2. Extent (in %) to Which Foreign Affiliates Are Staffed by Parent-Country Nationals (PCN), Host-Country Nationals (HCN), and Third-Country Nationals (TCN).

	U.S. MNCs	European MNCs	Japanese MNCs
United States			
Senior management PCN	NR[a]	29	83
Senior management HCN	NR	67	17
Senior management TCN	NR	4	0
Middle management PCN	NR	18	73
Middle management HCN	NR	82	27
Middle management TCN	NR	0	0
Lower management PCN	NR	4	40
Lower management HCN	NR	96	60
Lower management TCN	NR	0	0
Western Europe			
Senior management PCN	33	38	77
Senior management HCN	60	62	23
Senior management TCN	7	0	0
Middle management PCN	5	7	43
Middle management HCN	93	93	57
Middle management TCN	2	0	0
Lower management PCN	0	4	23
Lower management HCN	100	96	77
Lower management TCN	0	0	0
Canada			
Senior management PCN	25	28	33
Senior management HCN	74	67	67
Senior management TCN	1	5	0
Middle management PCN	1	11	33
Middle management HCN	99	89	67
Middle management TCN	0	0	0
Lower management PCN	3	0	17
Lower management HCN	96	100	83
Lower management TCN	1	0	0
Middle/Near East			
Senior management PCN	42	86	67
Senior management HCN	34	14	33
Senior management TCN	24	0	0
Middle management PCN	27	50	83
Middle management HCN	63	29	17
Middle management TCN	10	21	0
Lower management PCN	9	7	33
Lower management HCN	82	86	67
Lower management TCN	9	7	0

Table 1–2. *(continued)*

	U.S. MNCs	European MNCs	Japanese MNCs
Eastern Europe			
Senior management PCN	15.5	100	NR[b]
Senior management HCN	69	0	NR
Senior management TCN	15.5	0	NR
Middle management PCN	8	100	NR
Middle management HCN	92	0	NR
Middle management TCN	0	0	NR
Lower management PCN	0	100	NR
Lower management HCN	100	0	NR
Lower management TCN	0	0	NR
Latin/South America			
Senior management PCN	44	79	83
Senior management HCN	47	16	17
Senior management TCN	9	5	0
Middle management PCN	7	37	41
Middle management HCN	92	58	59
Middle management TCN	1	5	0
Lower management PCN	1	0	18
Lower management HCN	96	100	82
Lower management TCN	3	0	0
Far East			
Senior management PCN	55	85	65
Senior management HCN	38	15	35
Senior management TCN	7	0	0
Middle management PCN	19	25	41
Middle management HCN	81	75	59
Middle management TCN	0	0	0
Lower management PCN	2	5	18
Lower management HCN	96	95	82
Lower management TCN	2	0	0
Africa			
Senior management PCN	36	75	50
Senior management HCN	47	15	33
Senior management TCN	17	10	17
Middle management PCN	11	35	0
Middle management HCN	78	65	100
Middle management TCN	11	0	0
Lower management PCN	5	0	0
Lower management HCN	90	95	100
Lower management TCN	5	5	0

a. Data were collected on staffing policies of foreign affiliates only. Hence, no statistic was gathered for home country of MNC.

b. None of the Japanese MNCs included in this study has affiliate operations in Eastern Europe.

one would expect the more-developed nations to have a larger pool of personnel possessing the necessary manpower and technical skills to staff management-level positions. The Japanese MNCs, on the other hand, employ considerably more parent-country nationals in their overseas operations at the senior and middle management levels. The Japanese MNCs do not use third-country nationals at any level of management in their overseas affiliate operations, except in Africa.

Respondents were asked to identify the reasons for staffing overseas operations with parent-country, host-country, and third-country nationals. For the U.S. sample, the most important reasons mentioned for staffing with parent-country nationals and the relative frequencies with which the reasons were cited were to organize a foreign enterprise in the start-up phase (70 percent) and to ensure technical expertise (68 percent). The major reasons for staffing with host-country nationals were to benefit from their familiarity with the culture (83 percent), to benefit from their knowledge of the language (79 percent), to reduce costs (61 percent), and to achieve good public relations (58 percent). The most primary reasons for staffing with third-country nationals were to ensure technical expertise (55 percent) and because the third-country national was best person for the job (53 percent).

For the West European sample, the key reasons identified for staffing with parent-country nationals and the relative frequencies with which the reasons were cited were to enable the parent firm to develop an internationally oriented management for headquarters, where foreign assignments are seen as management development (69 percent); to ensure technical expertise (69 percent); and to organize a foreign enterprise in the start-up phase (68 percent). The most important reasons for staffing with host-country nationals were to benefit from their familiarity with the culture (72 percent) and knowledge of the language (69 percent). The primary reason for staffing with third-country nationals was that the third-country national was the best person for the job (53 percent). The respondents were mixed about the other reasons for employing third-country nationals.

For the Japanese sample, the most important reason for staffing with parent-country nationals and the relative frequency with which the reason was cited was that the parent-country national was the best person for the job (55 percent). All other reasons were considered relatively unimportant. The same held true for staffing with host-country nationals: the host-country national was the best person for the job (68 percent). Since

Japanese MNCs do not use third-country nationals in most of their foreign affiliates, no reason was given under this category.

Selection Criteria

In this study, overseas managerial assignments were classified into four major categories: the chief executive officer (CEO), whose responsibility is to oversee and direct the entire foreign operation; the functional head, whose job is to establish functional departments in a foreign subsidiary; the troubleshooter, whose function is to analyze and solve specific operational problems; and the operative. Jobs in each of these categories involve varying degrees of contact with the local culture and varying lengths of stay in any given country. One would expect a CEO to have more extensive contact with members of the local community than a troubleshooter, and the troubleshooter's job in a certain country to be of shorter duration than the CEO's. Given these differences, variations might appear in criteria used for selecting personnel in each of the job categories.

Analysis of variance showed that for the U.S. sample, the criteria used for selecting candidates in each of the job categories were significantly different at the .005 level. For each job category in the U.S. sample, certain criteria were considered more important than others. In jobs requiring more extensive contact with the local community (CEO and functional head), attributes like "adaptability," "flexibility in new environmental settings," and "good communication skills" were more frequently identified as being very important, compared to jobs that were more technically oriented (troubleshooter). For the West European and Japanese samples, the pattern was slightly different. The key criterion for selecting candidates in the CEO category in both samples was "managerial talent," and the most important criterion for selecting candidates in the functional head, troubleshooter, and operative categories was "technical knowledge of the business."

In the West European sample, adaptability/flexibility was considered a significant criterion in three of the four job categories: 77 percent of the respondents cited this as a very important criterion for jobs in the CEO category, 81 percent in the functional head category, and 62 percent in the troubleshooter category. "Interest in overseas work" was cited as a very important criterion for each of the four job categories by a majority of the firms, although not cited as frequently as the aforementioned criteria.

In addition to technical knowledge of business, most of the Japanese firms considered "experience in company" a very important criterion for jobs in three of the four job categories: 89 percent of the respondents identified this as a very important criterion for jobs in the CEO catgory, 71 percent for jobs in the functional head category, and 53 percent for jobs in the troubleshooter category. This criterion may reflect the system of employment in Japanese society, whereby only the most experienced individuals are considered for promotion to the CEO level. Adaptability/flexibility in new environmental settings was also cited as a very important criterion for each job category by a majority of the firms, although not cited as frequently as the aforementioned criteria. An interesting finding was that the candidate's gender was mentioned by over half of the West European and Japanese MNCs as a criterion used in all four job categories, but by none of the U.S. multinationals. This is probably attributable to differences among the countries in equal employment opportunities. The West European and Japanese MNCs were perhaps less inhibited in acknowledging that there are perceived problems in assigning women expatriates because of the attitude toward working women in some societies.

Selection Procedures

The study also examined the procedures undertaken by the firms to determine the candidate's suitability for an overseas position. To the question: "Are tests administered to determine the candidate's technical competence?" 3 percent, 5 percent, and 14 percent, respectively, in the U.S., Japanese, and West European samples replied in the affirmative. To the question: "Are tests administered to determine the candidate's relational abilities?" 5 percent of the U.S. firms and 21 percent of the West European firms said yes. None of the Japanese firms used such a test. The U.S. firms that tested the candidate's relational abilities described such tests as including judgment by seniors, psychological appraisal, and interviews by a consulting psychologist with both the candidate and the spouse. In the European sample, the most common screening device to determine the candidate's relational abilities was psychological testing, a method used more often by the West European MNCs than by their U.S. counterparts.

It is rather surprising that an overwhelming majority of the U.S. firms participating in the study failed to assess the candidate's relational abilities when they clearly recognize that relational abilities are important for overseas work, as evidenced by their responses to the "criteria for selection" section, and when research shows relational abilities to be crucial to success in overseas assignments (Hays 1971, 1974; Ivancevich 1969; Miller 1972). Given the increasing demand for personnel who can function effectively abroad and the relatively high incidence of failure, there certainly appears to be room for improvement in this area.

Regarding the Japanese sample, it is interesting to note that even though none of the firms administered tests to determine the candidate's relational abilities, the Japanese MNCs clearly recognize the importance of such skills to success in an overseas environment. As will be discussed later, 57 percent of the firms had specialized training programs to prepare candidates for overseas work.

The questionnaire respondents were asked to indicate whether interviews were conducted with the candidate alone or candidate and the spouse for managerial and technically oriented positions. In the U.S. sample, for managerial positions, 52 percent of the firms conducted interviews with both the candidate and the spouse, 47 percent conducted interviews with the candidate only, and 1 percent conducted no interviews. For technically oriented positions, 40 percent of the companies conducted interviews with both the candidate and the spouse, 59 percent with the candidate only, and 1 percent did not conduct interviews. The profile of West European MNCs is similar to that of the U.S. firms. For managerial positions, a full 41 percent of the companies interviewed both the candidate and the spouse, while the remaining 59 percent interviewed the candidate only. For technically oriented positions, 38 percent of the companies interviewed both the candidate and the spouse, while the remaining 62 percent interviewed the candidate only. These figures suggest that in managerial positions, which involve more extensive contact with the local community than do technically oriented positions, the adaptability of the spouse to living in a foreign environment was perceived as important for successful performance abroad. However, even for technically oriented positions, a sizable proportion of the firms conducted interviews with both the candidate and the spouse. This lends support to the contention of other researchers (Borrmann 1968; Harris and Harris 1972; Hays 1974) that MNCs are cognizant of the importance of adaptability to effective performance abroad. The study did not examine the nature of questions posed during these interviews. In general, these should be more probing than those asked in interviews for the average domestic position. Questions pertaining to the candidate's "marital relationships, prejudices, interpersonal relationships, and many other characteristics related to adjustment abroad'' should be asked to determine the person's suitability for an overseas position (Sieveking, Anchor, and Marston 1981: 201).

For the Japanese sample, 71 percent of the firms conducted interviews with the candidate only for managerial positions, and 62 percent conducted interviews with the candidate only for technically oriented positions. None of the firms included the spouse in interviews for positions in either category. This is strikingly different from both the U.S. and West European samples and could be attributed to the fact that Japanese culture has a different view of the spouse's (in this case, the wife's) role and status in the family. It should be noted, however, that given the unique characteristics of the Japanese system of personnel management, even though official interviews are not conducted with the candidate's spouse, the company is usually very familiar with the details of the employee's family situation. Consequently, the family situation is indirectly taken into consideration in the selection decision.

Training Programs

The analysis here will focus on those training programs designed to prepare personnel for cross-cultural encounters. The programs are listed in ascending order of rigor.

1. *Area studies programs* include environmental briefing and cultural orientation programs that provide the trainee with factual information about a particular country's sociopolitical history, stage of economic development, geography, climate, housing, schools, cultural institutions, and value systems.

2. *Culture assimilator programs* consist of a series of seventy-five to one hundred episodes briefly describing an intercultural encounter. The culture assimilator is based on the critical-incidents method, that is, presenting incidents determined (by a panel of experts, including returned expatriates) to be critical to the situation between members of two different cultures. Studies of the validity and effectiveness of this training method have shown that in general ''these programs provide an apparently effective method for assisting members of one culture to interact and adjust successfully with members of another culture'' (Fiedler and Mitchell 1971: 95). The technique, however,

was designed specifically for people who were assigned overseas on short notice. Consequently, when time is not a major factor, and when assignments will require extensive contact with members of the local community, this technique should be supplemented by more rigorous training programs.

3. *Language training programs* teach the candidate the language of the country to which he is assigned. It often takes months, sometimes years, for a candidate to master a foreign language.

4. *Sensitivity training programs* focus on learning at the affective level and are designed to develop the individual's attitudinal flexibility to make him aware, and eventually accept, that unfamiliar modes of behavior and value systems can be valid in their own cultures. Although the effectiveness of sensitivity sessions has been questioned, there is some indication that they may "well be a powerful technique in the reduction of ethnic prejudice, particularly among those who are low in psychological anomie" (Rubin 1967: 30). The Peace Corps is by far the most ardent advocate of this method of training. To increase the effectiveness of sensitivity training, the Peace Corps supplements these sessions with field experience.

5. *Field experience programs* send candidates to the country of assignment or to microcultures nearby (such as Indian reservations or urban black ghettos) where the trainees may experience some of the emotional stress of living and working with people from a different subculture. Research indicates that although differences in cultural content exist between these microcultures and the country to which the trainee is assigned, trainees seem to benefit from their encounters with people whose way of life is different from their own since "the process problems that grow out of confrontation are similar" (Harris and Harris 1972: 9).

In the U.S. sample, only 32 percent of the respondents indicated that their companies had formalized training programs to prepare candidates for overseas work; a full 68 percent offered no such programs. The reasons, and the relative frequencies with which the reasons were cited, for omitting training programs were that there is a trend toward employment of local nationals (45 percent), that the nature of such assignments is temporary (28 percent), that they doubt the effectiveness of such training programs (20 percent), and that they lack time (7 percent).

In contrast, 69 percent of the respondents in the West European sample sponsored training programs to prepare the candidates for overseas assignment. The reasons, and the relative frequencies with which the reasons were cited, for omitting training programs were that the nature of such assignments is temporary (30 percent), that they lack time (30 percent), that there is a trend toward employment of local nationals (20 percent) and that they doubt the effectiveness of such training programs (20 percent).

Fifty-seven percent of the Japanese MNCs responding had training programs to prepare candidates for overseas work. This is consistent with the survey findings of *Japan Economic News* (1982), which reported that 70 percent of the 267 largest Japanese multinationals provided some formal training programs to their expatriates prior to overseas assignment. For those firms that did not provide training, the reasons, and the relative frequencies with which the reasons were cited, for omitting training programs were that they lack time (63 percent) and doubt the effectiveness of such training programs (37 percent).

The firms that sponsored training were asked to indicate the types of programs they used for personnel in each of the four job categories. Table 1-3 presents the relative frequency with which a particular program was used for each of the job categories in all three samples. Results indicate that most of the U.S. and West European firms that had training programs recognized the need for more rigorous training for the CEOs and functional heads than for troubleshooters and operatives. In contrast, the Japanese firms provide slightly more rigorous training for operatives. This may arise from the fact that since Japanese CEOs have more extensive records of overseas work experience, there is less need to subject them to the more rigorous programs.

The firms that sponsored training programs were asked whether they evaluated the effectiveness of such training programs and, if so, to enumerate the types of evaluation procedures used. Thirty-two percent of the U.S. firms, 26 percent of the West European firms, and 33 percent of the Japanese firms adopted some form of evaluation process. For all three samples, procedures for evaluating the effectiveness of such training programs included both the trainees' and the supervisors' subjective evaluations.

Success and Reasons for Success

Respondents were asked to indicate the most important reasons for an expatriate's inability to function effectively in a foreign environment. For

Table 1–3. Frequency of Training Programs Used for Each Job Category in U.S., European, and Japanese Samples (in %).

Job Category	CEO			Functional Head			Trouble Shooter			Operative		
Training Programs	U.S.	Eur.	Jap.	U.S.	Eur.	Jap.	U.S.	Eur.	Jap.	U.S.	Eur.	Jap.
Environmental briefing	52	57	67	54	52	57	44	38	52	31	38	67
Cultural orientation	42	55	14	41	52	14	31	31	19	24	28	24
Cultural assimilator	10	21	14	10	17	14	7	10	14	9	14	19
Language training	60	76	52	59	72	57	36	41	52	24	48	76
Sensitivity training	3	3	0	1	3	0	1	3	5	0	3	5
Field experience	6	28	14	6	24	10	4	3	10	1	7	24

the U.S. sample, the reasons given in descending order of importance were the inability of the manager's spouse to adjust to a different physical or cultural environment; the manager's inability to adapt to a different physical or cultural environment; other family-related problems; the manager's personality or emotional maturity; the manager's inability to cope with the larger responsibilities posed by the overseas work; the manager's lack of technical competence for the job assignment; and the manager's lack of motivation to work overseas. These findings are in line with Hays' (1974) assertion that the family situation and relational abilities are responsible, in the main, for failure or poor performance abroad. In light of these findings, it appears all the more surprising that while most personnel administrators recognize the importance of these factors, the majority fail to take appropriate actions. Few companies actually pursue rigorous methods for assessing and developing the relational abilities of the expatriate personnel.

In the West European sample, responses were fairly mixed. Only one reason was mentioned by most firms as being important for explaining poor performance abroad: the inability of the manager's spouse to adjust to a different cultural or physical environment. Other possible reasons were perceived to have a marginal impact upon the expatriate's performance.

This could indicate either that the failure rate for European MNCs was very low (as was the case) or that the European MNCs were not aware of the reasons and potential reasons for failure. The findings of the in-depth interviews with 17 European multinationals presented in subsequent chapters shed further light on this issue.

For the Japanese sample, the reasons given in descending order of importance were the manager's inability to cope with the larger responsibilities posed by the overseas work; the manager's inability to adapt to a different physical or cultural environment; the manager's personality or emotional maturity; the manager's lack of technical competence for the job assignment; inability of the manager's spouse to adjust to a different physical or cultural environment; the manager's lack of motivation to work overseas; and other family-related problems. This ordering of reasons contrasts with that of the United States but does not come as a surprise. Rather, it reflects differences in the American and Japanese cultures regarding both the role of the spouse and systems of management. In Japan, decisions are arrived at through consensus. There is a strong sense of group cohesion, or "groupism," among Japanese managers. Overseas managers, however, find themselves fairly isolated from corporate headquarters. Although they maintain daily contact through the telephone or other means of telecommunications, they lack the close interaction that they enjoyed at home. Moreover, they are suddenly burdened with added responsibilities as overseas representatives, a role they are generally not accustomed to performing alone. In the words of one Japanese executive, some expatriates experience "status shock" (Tung 1984a).

Respondents were asked to indicate the percentage of expatriates that have to be recalled to their home country or dismissed because of inability to function effectively. For the U.S. sample, 7 percent of the respondents indicated that the recall or failure rate was 20 to 40 percent, 69 percent of the firms had a recall rate of 10 to 20 percent, and the remaining 24 percent had recall rates of below 10 percent. For the West European and Japanese samples, the failure rates were lower. Fifty-nine percent of the West European firms had recall rates lower than 5 percent; 38 percent had recall rates of 6 to 10 percent; and only 3 percent had failure rates of 11 to 15 percent. For the Japanese sample, 76 percent of the firms had failure or recall rates of below 5 percent; 10 percent had failure, or recall, rates of 6 to 10 percent; 14 percent had failure rates of 11 to 15 percent. There are two possible explanations for the lower failure rates of West European and Japanese firms: either their expatriates by nature, selection, and training are more adept at living and working in a foreign environment, or European

mechanisms in Japanese organizations are usually implicit rather than explicit (Pascale and Athos 1981). Thus it may be difficult for foreigners to gain an implicit understanding of the company's philosophy, which is central to smooth operations in industrial organizations.

4. Until recently, Japanese multinationals had problems in recruiting competent local nationals to work for their overseas subsidiaries.

5. Because of the system of lifetime employment and seniority, there may be a psychological reluctance among the Japanese to hire foreigners.

The Japanese are beginning to see advantages associated with the use of host-country nationals, and many of the manufacturing companies have established localization policies. However, problems remain in implementing such policies, many of which arise from the difficulty of incorporating local nationals into the Japanese industrial system (Matsuno and Stoever 1982; Tung 1984a).

While the policy of using host-country nationals is commendable and should be continued, U.S. and European multinationals should not rely solely on this source for staffing their overseas operations for three reasons. First, although local nationals can effectively manage their compatriots and relate well to domestic clients, they might have problems in communicating with corporate headquarters because of their unfamiliarity with overall corporate goals and objectives. Hence many U.S. and European MNCs recognize the need to post a number of expatriates as liaisons between the foreign subsidiary and corporate headquarters (Tung 1984a). This was apparently one of the reasons for IBM's decision to send more than two hundred expatriates to Japan in early 1985. Second, with the increasing trend toward the globalization of industries, managers need to possess an international outlook in their decision-making and problem-solving. This international perspective can be developed through overseas job assignments. Given the importance placed on international markets, most European multinationals consider expatriate assignments a significant part of a manager's overall career development. U.S. multinationals should adopt a similar policy. Third, with the increasing cooperation among nations in business transactions and activities, the number of individuals who will be sent overseas in the years ahead will rise. In light of these developments, and given the higher rates of expatriate failure among U.S. multinationals, attempts should be made to improve present selection criteria and training programs for overseas work.

Failure and Reasons for Failure

The statistics that emerged from the research survey for U.S. multinationals were fairly dismal. The principal reasons for failure are the expatriates' lack of relational skills (their inability, as individuals, to deal effectively with clients, business associates, superiors, peers, and subordinates in a foreign environment) and problematic family situations. The latter reason was also true for the European MNCs. The study highlights the crucial role of the family situation to successful expatriate performance in both the U.S. and West European samples. This points to the need to assess candidates' spouses in determining the candidates' suitability for overseas work and to include spouses in training programs that prepare them for living in a different cultural environment. Children, generally more flexible and adaptable by nature, probably do not need to be included in such programs.

The rank ordering of reasons for failure by Japanese MNCs was very different from those cited by their U.S. and European counterparts. In Japan's case, the manager's inability to cope with the larger responsibilities posed by the overseas work emerged as the most important factor for failure. This stems from the unique characteristics of the Japanese management system.

Selection Criteria and Procedures

Despite the recognition among U.S. personnel administrators that the family situation and lack of relational skills are often responsible for an expatriate's inability to function effectively in a foreign environment, they failed to place sufficient emphasis on these criteria. Many based their selection decisions primarily on technical competence, for two possible reasons. First, since it is difficult to identify and measure attitudes appropriate for cross-national interaction, it is easier to focus on the task-related variables. Second, Miller (1972) found that almost all of the personnel administrators he interviewed adopted a "minimax" decision strategy, one that would minimize the personal risks in selecting a candidate who might fail on the job. Since technical competence almost always prevents immediate failure on the job, the selectors play it safe by heavily emphasizing technical qualifications. This practice of basing the selection decision on technical competence alone, regardless of country of foreign assignment, may account for the high failure rate among expatriates in U.S. multinationals (Hays 1971; Howard 1974; Tung 1981).

A larger percentage of the European MNCs surveyed administered tests to determine the candidate's abilities to adapt to foreign environments. Furthermore, given the smaller size of the European nations, most Europeans have greater exposure to and contact with people of other countries. This heightens their awareness of cross-cultural differences and makes them more adaptable to foreign environments.

Although the Japanese multinationals did not administer specific tests to determine a candidate's relational abilities, these abilities were clearly taken into consideration in the selection decision (Tung 1984a). Further-more, most Japanese MNCs recognize the importance of such skills to success abroad, as evidenced by the fact that 57 percent of the firms studied here and 70 percent of the 267 largest Japanese multinationals surveyed by the *Japan Economic News* (1982) had specialized training programs to prepare candidates for overseas work.

Training Programs

The five types of training programs listed in the analysis section of this chapter focus on different kinds of learning (cognitive versus affective) and vary in terms of medium of instruction, information content, and time and resources required. These programs are by no means mutually exclusive; rather, they should be complementary and seen as part of a continuum ranging from low to high rigor (from environmental briefing to sensitivity training and field experiences). Depending on the job and the country of foreign assignment, the individual should be involved in one or several of these programs.

In the U.S. sample, only 32 percent of the respondents indicated that their company had formal training programs to prepare candidates for overseas work. Most of these firms used environmental briefings designed to provide the trainee with information about a particular country's sociopolitical history, geography, stage of economic development, and cultural institutions. The assumption behind this approach is that "knowl-edge will increase empathy, and empathy will modify behavior in such a way as to improve intercultural relationships" (Campbell 1969: 3). Although there is some indication that increased knowledge removes some of the fear and aggression aroused by the unknown, the evidence that knowledge will invariably result in increased empathy is sparse and usually not the result of rigorous experimental control. In fact, some evidence indicates that the understanding and endorsement of a different culture are not necessarily linked (Useem, Useem, and Donoghue 1963; Deutsch 1970). When used alone, environmental briefings are inadequate to prepare trainees for assignments that require extensive contact with the local community overseas (Textor 1966; Harrison and Hopkins 1967; Lynton and Pareek 1967). Furthermore, since there can be numerous cultural differences between two countries, training programs of this nature cannot possibly impart all the knowledge that will be required over the duration of trainees' assignments. Given the financial resources available to international corporations and the ready accessibility to microcultures at home, MNCs should introduce more rigorous training programs. The field experience of living and working with members of a microculture need not necessitate prolonged absence from the company. Often a week-long live-in experience will be sufficient to expose candidates to the emotional strain of living with members of a different culture.

In contrast, 69 percent of the European multinationals and 57 percent of the Japanese firms surveyed had training programs to prepare candidates for overseas work. The Japanese provide more rigorous programs with an emphasis on language training and interacting with foreign nationals. (In the case of U.S. multinationals, language training is less important since English is the lingua franca of international commerce.) Most Japanese MNCs also sponsor programs to prepare candidates for interaction with members of a foreign culture, such as teaching the host country's history and social traditions and sponsoring exchanges in which Caucasians live with the Japanese trainees, giving the trainees ample opportunity to practice their language skills and learn foreign ways. There is certainly room for improvement for U.S. multinationals in this regard.

Relationship between Selection, Training and Incidence of Success

The data on the U.S. sample provide support for the contingency framework for human resource planning developed by Tung (1981). The contingency model states essentially that given the differences in degrees of contact required with the local culture, the varying durations of stay in the foreign country, and the varying degrees of differences between the home and other foreign cultures, no one selection criterion should be emphasized and no one training program should be used, regardless of the task and environment. Rather, the contingency framework allows for the systematic analysis of variations in task and environmental factors. Due to the variability of each situation in terms of country of foreign assignment and the task to be performed, constant weights applicable to all instances cannot be assigned to each of these factors. A more feasible strategy is to adopt a contingency approach to the selection of personnel for overseas assignments.

This approach requires a clear identification of the task, the environment, and the psychological characteristics of the individual under consideration. A first step in the selection process is to identify the job. Here, the administrator should assess how much interaction with the local community the position will require. Jobs in the CEO and functional head categories generally call for more extensive contacts with the community; hence such jobs rank high in terms of degree of interaction. A second set of factors relates to the environment. Here, the magnitude of differences between the political, legal, socioeconomic, and cultural systems of the home country and the host nation should be assessed and rank ordered. Data on such differences are readily available from research and educational institutions in the United States, such as the International Data Library and Reference Service at the University of California at Berkeley and the Cross-National Data Archive Holdings at Indiana University, Bloomington.

The multinational should ascertain whether a candidate is willing to serve overseas. No training program can change the attitude of an individual opposed to serving abroad. In the opinion of several European executives, the candidate must be adventurous and eager to explore the unknown. Otherwise, the assignment is doomed to failure. If the individual is willing to live and work in a foreign environment, the company should assess the extent to which he is tolerant of cultural differences and his ability to work toward intercultural cooperation. Howard (1974: 140-141) identified a list of appraisal methods (including psychometric devices) that can be used to determine the individual's capacity for tolerance of foreign customs, cultures, and business practices. These include the Minnesota Multiphasic Personality Inventory, the Guilford-Zimmerman Temperament Survey, the Allport-Vernon Study of Values, the F-test (a psychiatric evaluation), and evaluations from superiors, subordinates, friends, and acquaintances.

In addition, personnel administrators should consider an alternative source of human power—local nationals. Most of the 80 U.S. multinationals surveyed appeared to realize the advantages associated with staffing overseas subsidiaries with local nationals, but they differed in the extent to which they used local nationals at various levels of management. The firms did use local nationals to a much greater extent and at all levels of management, in developed countries than in less-developed nations. This is not surprising; the more-developed nations have a larger pool of personnel with the necessary skills to staff executive-level positions. The countries staffed by a smaller percentage of local nationals at management levels of U.S. subsidiaries tend to be ones whose culture, values, and business practices diverge more from those in the United States.

The selection-decision process can be illustrated by means of a flowchart (see Figure 1–1). Before headquarters launches a search at home for an appropriate individual to fill an overseas position, it should ask whether the job could be filled by a local national. If the answer is yes, this alternative should be considered. If the position cannot be filled by a local national, a search must be conducted among those with domestic operations or within competing industries.

The first step in the process is to identify the degree of interaction with the local community the job entails. In positions requiring extensive contact with the culture and an understanding of the local value system, relational abilities and environmental variables should be dominant factors in the selection decision. The selector should then examine the degree to which the foreign environment differs from that of the home country. If the differences are insignificant, the selection should be based primarily on task variables. Where the differences are great, the decision could focus on relational abilities and the family situation. In Figure 1–1 the family situation factor is categorized with the relational abilities factor because research has not yet determined how much effect the spouse has on the employee's performance.

The rest of the flow chart is self-explanatory. Expatriate training programs vary in their emphasis on the ability to relate to foreigners. If a job requires a great deal of interaction with the local community, and if the differences between the two cultures are great, the candidate should be involved in all five kinds of training programs, with particular emphasis on types 4 and 5. If contact with the local community is minimal, such as in a troubleshooter's job, and if the differences between the culture are small, the area studies program would probably be sufficient. Between these extremes lies a continuum of situations requiring varying degrees of

Figure 1–1. Flow Chart of the Selection-Decision Process.

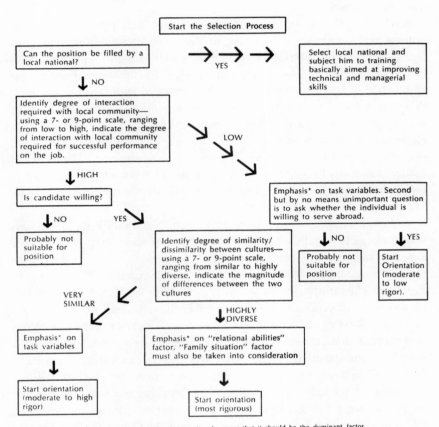

* "Emphasis" does not mean ignoring the other factors. It only means that it should be the dominant factor.

contact with the local culture and involving varying magnitudes of difference between the cultures. Personnel administrators should locate the job under consideration along this continuum and determine a suitable training program.

Moderate relationships were found between the use of appropriate criteria and incidence of success in the European sample, while no significant relationship was found in the Japanese sample. This highlights the key role that cultural differences play in the development and application of conceptual paradigms. As compared with Japan, the United States and West Europe are culturally more similar, which may account for the greater similarity observed among U.S. and European MNCs. However, even here we observe some differences in practices and outcomes. This finding points to the need to test empirically theories and models that apply to one culture before transferring them to other countries with substantially different cultures, even if the economic systems may be fairly similar.

Although the relationship between selection and incidence of success was moderately significant in the European sample and insignificant in the Japanese sample, in all three samples, it was found that the use of rigorous training programs could significantly improve an expatriate's performance overseas. Thus it appears all the more important for U.S. multinationals to provide comprehensive training for their expatriates.

To gain a better understanding of the reasons for the lower failure rates of European and Japanese MNCs, interviews were conducted with a sample of European and Japanese MNCs engaged in various industries. For the 17 European and 18 Japanese corporations surveyed, the failure rate nowhere exceeded 6 percent and 5 percent, respectively. In addition, interviews were conducted with personnel in three educational institutes that train expatriates for overseas assignments: the Center for International Briefing, Farnham Castle (U.K.); the Institute for International Studies and Training, which operates under the auspices of the Japanese Ministry of International Trade and Industry (Japan); and the International Education Center (Japan). These studies provide insight into the human resource planning and development programs among a sample of European and Japanese multinationals. The findings of the Japanese multinationals have been reported in my earlier book entitled *Key to Japan's Economic Strength: Human Power* (1984a). This book will focus on the human resource policies and practices among the sample of 17 European MNCs using the findings of the Japanese sample for comparative purposes.

2 TRAINING INSTITUTES FOR INTERNATIONAL ASSIGNMENTS

One frequently cited reason for the lower rate of expatriate failure among European and Japanese multinationals is the greater emphasis these corporations place on formal training to prepare candidates for the emotional and physical strains associated with assignments to exotic countries. The in-depth interviews with the European and Japanese MNCs included in this study revealed that the majority of firms from both samples sponsor formal training programs for their expatriates, the Japanese programs being more extensive in scope and intensive in nature. This chapter examines the types of programs offered by institutes in two countries, namely, the Center for International Briefing, Farnham Castle (U.K.), the Institute for International Studies and Training (Japan), and the Japanese American Conversation Institute (Japan).

THE CENTER FOR INTERNATIONAL BRIEFING, FARNHAM CASTLE (U.K.)

Information on the history and types of training programs offered by the Center for International Briefing was obtained from in-depth interviews with Patrick Lloyd, director, and Alan Hall, deputy director and course organizer for the Asia and Pacific regions. For twenty-seven years prior to joining the center, Lloyd worked with Shell Corporation, and had postings in London, Hong Kong, Spain, and Peru.

History and Objectives

The Center for International Briefing, a private organization, was founded in 1953 and is housed in an eleventh-century castle. The center was established to prepare people from various professions, occupations, such as business people, missionaries, and military personnel, for living abroad by educating them about the cultural characteristics in host-country societies. It offers environmental briefing programs on four major regions: Asia and the Pacific, Africa, the Middle East, and Latin America and the Caribbean. Briefings are not provided for West Europe, North America, and Australia because it is assumed that the living and working conditions in these countries are similar enough to those in the United Kingdom that they should not pose adjustment problems for the expatriate. Briefings, known as the "overseas regional courses," are the most popular programs offered by the center. Programs on each of the four geographic regions are given from nine to ten times a year, for an annual offering of thirty-six to forty overseas regional courses.

While the specific content of the various regional courses differs, all of the courses revolve around three main themes.

1. *Understanding the region.* The course examines the historical, political, religious, and economic factors that shape the culture of a given region. For the Middle East, for example, it investigates the affects and conditioning of Islam on people's behavior, response, and attitude toward life, work, family, age, education, and women and, most important, their attitude toward expatriates or foreigners who live among them.

2. *Understanding the individual countries.* After exposing the trainee to the general characteristics of a given geographic region, the program focuses on the subregion and the specific country to which the trainee is assigned. This is a key part of the program since the differences among the countries within a region can be significant and substantial. For example, an individual about to undertake an assignment in Japan would be enrolled in the Asia and Pacific overseas regional course. This region is, in turn, divided into four subgroups: East Asia, Southeast Asia, South Asia, and the Pacific. The person would join the East Asia subgroup and then choose the sessions in it that focus specifically on Japan.

3. *Understanding the social, domestic, and work environments in the host country.* The center does not offer vocational training but prepares the expatriate to adjust to all aspects of the environment (social, domestic, and occupational) in the destination country. "We don't teach a doctor to be a better physician professionally," explained Patrick Lloyd, "but we do provide the individual with the wherewithal to be a better doctor in Nepal, Sri Lanka, Indonesia, or Botswana, or wherever he is going. Through an understanding of the people of the destination country and their system of values and the cultural environment, we help him to prepare to adjust in

a very practical way [vis-á-vis climate, housing, servants and the proper attitude toward them, etc.] both in the work situation and in his personal life.'' The courses are designed to offer practical advice on virtually all matters that may arise in living in a foreign country, including salutation protocol, health care, and survival tips for subtropical and tropical climates.

The purpose of the overseas regional course is to ''make other countries interesting,'' to quote Hall, ''so that course members realize that people are what they are because of their experiences, background, history, creed, and the whole network or web of circumstances surrounding their lives. It makes it interesting and real, so that you can appreciate where you are. You are in somebody else's cultural zone. If you go there sticking out like a sore thumb, you get other people annoyed with you. They may not show it [this is another trap, of course] because people in Southeast Asia, for example, would not show it. The course members have got to know that too.'' It is crucial to understand this characteristic because in countries such as Japan and China, people generally do not openly display their displeasure with the actions and words of a foreign national. An expatriate's unintentional blunder may effectively terminate relationships or even negotiations with them.

The diversity of occupational backgrounds of the participants in an overseas regional course may pose problems in designing a curriculum that meets everyone's requirements. For that reason, the center offers concurrent sessions that cater to specific occupational interests. For example, the twenty-one participants enrolled in a regional briefing program are divided into eight groups, averaging three people or less to a group. Discussions are more narrowly focused in each work group, where participants can explore in depth the issues pertinent to their professional and personal interests in the foreign country. According to Hall, ''We do tailor-make the course to suit the individual, although people sometimes have difficulty believing it. We don't draw up the course program until we know who is in it, and then the courses are put together with them in mind.'' This custom designing is feasible because the center relies primarily on outside instructors for staffing its courses. Only those instructors who have expertise in subjects of interest to the group are recruited for a specific program. The outside instructors are drawn from the academic, business, and government sectors, including returned expatriates and foreign nationals. For a five-day residential program, typically sixty outside experts are brought in, at various times, to address the participants on a multitude of subjects.

The center trains approximately one thousand people every year, half of whom come from the United Kingdom. The remaining participants come from other European countries, with an occasional few from the United States. Many of the European MNCs studied currently use or plan to use the facilities at Farnham Castle. Spouses generally attend the program as well as the candidates themselves. As noted in Chapter 1, the inability of the spouse or the family to adjust to a foreign country is a primary reason for expatriate failure among both U.S. and European multinationals. To help offset such problems, many companies make an effort to include the spouses in their cross-cultural training programs. As of January 1, 1986, the cost per participant was 545 pounds, inclusive of accommodations and meals. Participants are generally between thirty and forty years of age.

In addition to the overseas regional courses, the center offers other types of training programs: the cultural awareness course, project briefings, business seminars, and the course on Britain. The cultural awareness course is designed for people who will eventually take up duties abroad but who do not yet know in which specific country or region. The purpose of this course is to heighten the individual's awareness to cultural differences in general, not to impart factual information on a particular country or region. In these sessions, the trainee is taught that a person's behavioral pattern, values, and attitudes are products of the unique cultural and environmental milieu in which that person is raised. The instructor sketches out a hypothetical situation and shows how a typical European responds to it. This is then contrasted with how a foreigner would respond under a similar set of circumstances. The differing behavioral patterns are then analyzed within the varying cultural contexts. The trainees are "made aware of their own situation within their own culture and are encouraged to see themselves as a product of their own culture," Hall explained. "They are then shown other circumstances where people who have arisen out of their cultures behave in certain ways. The message is that their [the foreigner's] behavior and attitude are just as valid for them as yours [British] are for you. Therefore, it is useless, stupid, unnecessary, and beside the point to say that this is *better* than that; it is merely *different*. They are brought to understand these differences." The cultural awareness course performs a function similar to that of the sensitivity training sessions described in Chapter 1. It is offered from three to eight times a year, depending upon demand, with an average of twenty to twenty-five participants per offering. This course is also a five-day residential program.

Project briefings and business seminars are programs custom designed by the Center for International Briefing to meet the specific requirements of a company. For example, the center can design a program to address a corporation's problems in launching a particular product in a given foreign country. The minimum number of participants for these tailor-made programs is fifteen.

Finally, the center offers the "Course about Britain," a program designed for foreign nationals who take up permanent or long-term residence in Britain. Here, participants learn about British culture and the specifics of the British way of life.

Mediums of Instruction

Each regional overseas program begins with an "ice-breaker" session in which participants are introduced to one another. The center refrains from training on the first day to allow participants to settle into the new physical surroundings and to become acquainted with their fellow trainees. Furthermore, since many trainees have been out of school for some while, they generally need time to get reacclimated to an educational setting.

A variety of mediums convey the themes covered in the regional overseas course, including lectures, panel discussions, seminars, and audio-visual presentations. Critical incidents are seldom used in the overseas regional courses; the center's administration believes that adults who have long been away from formal schooling do not respond well to this method of instruction. The method is, however, an important component of the center's cultural awareness program.

The regional overseas course is designed as an experiential learning exercise, somewhat like the Peace Corps' micro-cultures technique, along three different dimensions. The trainees are immersed in the culture of the destination region or country throughout the entire program. In addition, they live and interact with people from different occupational and educational backgrounds, thus, experientially learning to understand other viewpoints. Finally, the trainees are "shut in by the walls of the castle," thus remaining quite isolated from the outside world for the duration of the program. There is little or no opportunity for them to leave the castle grounds since the sessions are conducted from morning through late evening. The ambience of the eleventh-century castle in which the center is housed accentuates the "foreignness" of the situation. These three factors, in combination, require the trainees to adapt mentally and physically to a new environment, simulating the reality they will undergo in a foreign country. In sum, the week-long residential program creates a truly unique living experience for the trainees.

Trainees are encouraged to spend what spare time they have in the center's resource library, which has a rich collection of maps, books, and other literature on the various countries for which courses are offered. In addition, the library holds a compendium of letters written by expatriates who had attended the programs. These letters, filled with anecdotal accounts of daily situations the expatriates encountered while working abroad, are very insightful and useful to current trainees. Vera Attwood, an assistant to Hall, indicated that trainees often complain that they lack adequate time to consume the wealth of information contained in the library.

Evaulation of Program Effectiveness

At the end of the five-day residential program, trainees are required to evaluate the course's quality and effectiveness. In addition, many center graduates who are now abroad continue to write with suggestions for improving the program. The center takes all of these comments seriously. According to Lloyd, "We are self-critical all the time. We are constantly modifying. It is a continuous, dynamic process." Furthermore, the center works closely with the business sector to identify and serve the special needs of companies in the areas of expatriate assignments and overseas business projects.

Attwood noted that many participants have requested the center to provide language training along with its other courses. Hall indicated that while he encourages the participants to learn the host-country language, it is difficult to incorporate that component into the program because of the inordinate amount of time required for effective teaching of a foreign language.

Some General Observations on Expatriate Assignments

When asked to proffer some reasons for the low failure rates among British and other European MNCs, Hall ascribed the Europeans' better perform- ance to two factors: one, attitudinal differences between Americans and

Europeans and, two, the foreign language proficiency of most Europeans. In Hall's opinion, "Americans are more demanding. They are more satisfied with their own society — they believe that America is *the* best, and therefore they are judging other countries from the standpoint of America." The European superiority complex, in contrast, has been mellowed by a crisis in confidence over the past four decades. Prior to World War II, Europe viewed itself as the center of the universe. "Now we are beginning to realize that we are not. People know that, so they go out humbler than the average American." In the case of the United Kingdom, Hall asserted that since World War II, the British have suffered a "humbling or sobering experience." Britain has lost its status as a very powerful country with a vast worldwide empire and has declined economically as well. As a result, the Britons, along with the Europeans, are "much more realistic" in their attitude and approach to foreign countries. There is no parallel experience for the Americans. In his opinion, while Vietnam gave the United States a shock, it was "a different sort of shock"; economically, the United States is still in the forefront. Consequently, Americans still think "they can do things in other countries the way they feel they *should* be done. They try to change other people's ways." He, as well as many of the European executives interviewed for this study, considered this attitudinal difference a key reason for the inability of many Americans to work effectively abroad.

A second reason for the lower failure rate among British and European expatriates is their greater language facility. Most Europeans understand the need to learn other languages. "You are halfway there if you realize the need to learn the foreign language," asserted Hall. You have got to realize that you have to adapt to get on there. So you have the right attitude to begin with; whereas if you feel that English is the language, you are saying in fact that 'I am what I am' and then expect *other people* to adapt— you can't win with that attitude." This theme was echoed by virtually all the European executives interviewed for this study.

INSTITUTE FOR INTERNATIONAL STUDIES AND TRAINING (JAPAN)

The information on the history and types of educational programs offered by the Institute for International Studies and Training (IIST) was obtained from an in-depth interview with Shoichi Ohmagari, director of the IIST Overseas Program, unless otherwise stated.

History and Objectives

A striking characteristic of the Japanese industrial scene is the common objectives and ethos shared by the government, big business, and labor, giving the impression that the three sectors move in unison as one giant monolith. James Abegglen, a long-time observer of Japan, has referred to this characterization as "Japan Incorporated." Although this notion has been challenged on the grounds that big companies do not always comply with the wishes of the government (Tung 1984a; Tung 1986), business and government generally do tend to share a common set of objectives, one of which is international competitiveness.

Under the protection of the government, the Japanese economy recovered rapidly from the devastating effects of World War II, and by the mid- to late-1950s, Japan sought to assume the status of a leading economic power by playing a major role in the world trade system. Besides gaining membership to international financial and economic organizations, such as the General Agreement on Trade and Tariffs and the International Monetary Fund, and adopting procedures to liberalize both inward and outward capital investments, the country recognized its need to develop a pool of leaders in international business. Consequently, in 1967 the government enacted special legislation authorizing the establishment of the IIST to "provide graduate-level training for selected qualified persons contemplating careers in the international field," with the ultimate goal of developing "a body of rising young leaders who will eventually play a key role in international affairs" (IIST 1980–81).

The institute was established through initial funding from the government and business sectors. It continues to receive financial support from the Ministry of International Trade and Industry (MITI) and members of the Japan Federation of Economic Organization; tuition fees typically account for only 40 percent of the institute's revenue. The campus, located at the foot of Mt. Fuji, provides both classroom and dormitory facilities for trainees and faculty. In principle, the trainees live in dormitories, but married trainees usually go home on weekends since the institute does not provide housing for spouses.

Although the institute operates under the auspices of MITI, members of its board of governors are drawn primarily from large business corporations. The trainees are career staff from a diverse range of government agencies and business organizations, which pay their tuition fees and expenses in addition to their full-time salaries.

Every year the institute educates from 150 to 200 trainees. All of the participants are college graduates with approximately five to six years of experience in government or business; their average age is thirty. There are two types of programs: the regular program, which runs for the entire year, and the practical trade program, which spans a period of three months. The primary purpose of the regular program, which is country specific, is to train generalists and international businesspeople. A trainee whose assignment would be to the United States, for instance, studies English, U.S. management practices, U.S. history, and various aspects of American society. The three-month program is designed to train specialists. In the practical trade program, which is not necessarily country-oriented, only English and international business transactions courses are taught. When it was first established, this program was intended for small enterprises. Since the energy crisis of the early 1970s, however, many large companies have reduced the number of new career staff hired annually and consequently cannot send their employees to the institute for a year since they need them to staff the office. Thus, the three-month program is becoming increasingly popular with these companies.

The institute sponsors faculty and student exchanges with foreign universities. In addition to the fifteen full-time regular faculty members who teach courses in Japanese and foreign languages and Japanese culture, each year the institute invites approximately two hundred instructors from various educational institutions, both domestic and foreign, on a part-time basis. Usually eight of these visiting professors are invited from the United States, Canada, France, United Kingdom, and other developed nations to teach courses in international management and economics. When asked whether the extensive use of part-time faculty from abroad poses problems in terms of lack of continuity and diversity of standards, Ohmagari responded it should not. The visiting professors sign contracts one year in advance, at which time they are invited to the campus and provided with information about teaching in the institute. Furthermore, most of the visiting faculty are drawn from IIST's affiliate universities overseas. Consequently, those who have already taught at the center can share information with their colleagues who will be teaching at the IIST the following year.

The institute has formal exchange programs with the American University and the American Graduate School of Management in the United States, the Euro-Japanese Exchange Foundation Study Center in the United Kingdom, and Institut Européen d'Administration des Affaires (INSEAD) in France. In addition to inviting faculty from these universities, the institute also schedules student exchanges. Every spring, some forty to fifty exchange students from IIST's affiliate institutes in the United States, Canada, and France spend four months on campus. Living with these foreign students over a four-month period provides the Japanese trainees with an opportunity to practice their foreign-language skills and learn first-hand about the culture, values, and attitudes characteristic of various foreign countries. In addition, it heightens their awareness to cross-cultural differences and helps them acquire the skills needed to adapt to foreign nationals. The purpose served by the live-in programs is similar to the field experience mechanism described in Chapter 1.

Regular Program

The objective of the regular program, which enrolls eighty people annually, is to train businesspeople who will work in the international arena. The curriculum is divided into four parts: foreign language, international management and economics, area studies, and overseas training.

Many Japanese MNCs consider language an important criterion in the selection of a candidate for overseas assignment since Japanese is seldom used outside of Japan. Although Japanese schoolchildren study English from grade seven on, the emphasis is on reading and writing, not on conversing. Many Japanese believe this method of instruction has made them poor linguists and accounts for their difficulties in conveying their thoughts to non-Japanese (*Nippon* 1982: 153).

For this reason, the regular program emphasizes language training. The number of instructional hours required for training in English language has been increased from 240 to 540, excluding the courses in international management and economics, which are conducted in English. English language is taught in the first eight weeks of the program by native speakers, who focus on improving their students' listening and speaking skills. The trainees are divided into small groups based on their competence in English. In addition to learning the language through formal lectures and laboratory training, the trainees are given ample opportunity to practice their English with Caucasian exchange students.

The next segment of the program extends for twenty-two weeks and offers courses in international management and economics, area studies, and Japanese studies. The courses in international management and economics are designed to provide trainees with skills in these functional disciplines so that they will be prepared to handle the broader duties associated with working abroad. As noted in Chapter 1, a principal reason for failure among Japanese expatriates is their inability to cope with the larger responsibilities associated with an overseas position. Consequently, knowledge in the functional disciplines is considered essential.

The area studies program provides the knowledge trainees will require for living in the geographic region to which they may be assigned. The program consists of two parts, and each trainee selects one geographic region from each section. The first section includes North America and Western Europe, and the second section covers the socialist bloc nations, the Middle and Near East, Latin and South America, and Southeast Asia. The trainee studies the history, culture, and socioeconomic and political characteristics of each region as well as its relationship with Japan. Although the course content is primarily factual, the program stresses adaptation and interaction with members of a foreign culture. As Ohmagari noted, "This is particularly important for us Japanese people who live in a small, isolated homogeneous society. We do not know how to deal with foreigners, who have different cultures. So, the major purpose of our program is to teach the trainees how to adapt to the local environment once they are overseas."

The curriculum consists of lectures by overseas instructors, foreign case studies, interaction with foreign exchange students, and seminar discussions with guest speakers, among them ambassadors and ministers, foreign businessmen living in Japan, and overseas researchers. The seminars provide the trainees with an opportunity to interact with experienced practitioners from other nations. The trainees are also taught about Japanese society, Japan's position in the world economic system, and how to explain the distinguishing characteristics of Japanese society and culture to non-Japanese. Students in the program go to classes from 9 A.M. to 4 P.M., attend seminars in the evenings, then turn to homework and other preparation for the following day's lectures. According to Ohmagari, most of them study until 2 A.M., reflecting the general diligence and dedication of Japanese employees to their companies.

In addition to the above-mentioned exchange students from advanced nations, the institute invites fifteen participants from developing countries to attend the Japanese studies program for four weeks. These participants are either university professors or members of the government or business communities. Their interactions with the trainees are particularly useful since Japanese investments in the developing nations, especially in the Far East, are very extensive.

The third section of the regular program is devoted to eight weeks of another foreign language, such as Spanish or German, or advanced English. The selection of the language is based on the country or region to which the trainee will be assigned.

The fourth section focuses on overseas training. Participation in this segment is entirely voluntary and involves four weeks of study in one of the following institutions abroad: the American University and the American Graduate School of Management in the United States, INSEAD in France, and the Euro-Japanese Exchange Foundation Study Center in the United Kingdom. This program provides an opportunity for the participants to live in the foreign country to which they may later be assigned and to associate with experts and businesspeople there.

In 1982, the tuition and expenses for the program amounted to roughly 6,332,900 yen. Although the dollar amount a company spends on each trainee is high, the Japanese system of lifetime employment virtually guarantees that it is a safe investment. The willingness of corporations to spend large sums on each career employee's education reflects the overall commitment of both the private and public sectors to international development.

Practical Trade Program

The three-month program focuses on the practical aspects of doing business abroad, specifically international business transactions, foreign exchange management, and foreign investment (IIST 1982). English is also taught. The program is not country oriented and does not include an area studies program, as does the regular program.

The first six weeks of the program are devoted to English-language training. The objectives and mediums of instruction are similar to those of the regular program; the difference is in the number of hours spent. In the three-month program, every trainee spends 230 hours learning English, as compared to 540 hours for the regular program. The trainees in the three-month program also share the dormitory with foreign exchange students to enable them to practice their English skills and to learn more about foreign cultures. The participants in the three-month program attend the same evening seminar discussions.

The second part of the practical trade program focuses on developing skills in English correspondence; the objective is to help trainees write "business English with genuine English expressions rather than Japanese English" (IIST 1982).

The third part of the program concentrates on intercultural communication, fostered through an understanding of the culture from which English expressions arise. Without comprehending the cultural roots behind the development of many idiomatic expressions, a non-native speaker of English simply cannot develop a good command of the language.

The fourth part of the program deals with practical training in the areas of international business transactions, foreign exchange management, international trade, trade administration regulations, documentation, and marketing abroad. Again, the format includes lectures, case studies, and seminars.

Enrollment in the practical trade program is limited to seventy participants per semester. All trainees are sponsored by their respective organizations, which pay all tuition fees and expenses, in addition to the trainees' regular wages. In 1982 the expenses for the three-month program amounted to approximately 809,700 yen.

Evaluation of Program Effectiveness

Upon completion of either program, trainees are asked to evaluate its effectiveness in preparing them for overseas work. In addition, the institute periodically invites personnel managers from major Japanese companies to review the program and offer suggestions for improvement. This information provides guidelines for modifying the program to meet the needs of government and industry better.

When asked about possible changes that may be made to the program, Ohmagari indicated that he would like to expand the exchange programs by inviting more foreign students and visiting professors. He further noted that the institute would like to include foreign participants with work experience, but this may not be possible because it is difficult for foreign companies to grant extended leaves of absence to their employees.

Some General Observations on Expatriate Assignments

Ohmagari was also asked to comment on various aspects of expatriate assignments. When asked to proffer some reasons for the low failure rates among Japanese MNCs, he mentioned three factors. The first is management education programs, such as those offered by his institute and other agencies. Second is the long-term perspective adopted by most Japanese companies. Ohmagari estimated that most Japanese firms spend at least three years investigating overseas market opportunities before they enter a particular country. This analysis increases their understanding of consumers' needs and preferences and of the nature of competition in the foreign country, thus greatly reducing the possibility of failure overseas (Tung 1984a). Third, given the practice of lifetime employment, employees have a strong sense of loyalty and commitment to the company; in turn, the employers have an overarching concern for the employees. "[Japanese] companies do not expect short-term returns" Ohmagari noted. "In other words, the company views the market from a long-range point of view. They earn profit over a decade or so. They don't expect to earn profits overnight. This is very different from the American mentality. The most important concern of American firms is profit. In contrast, Japanese firms are most concerned with maintaining their employees."

When asked to identify the criteria most often used by Japanese MNCs in selecting employees for overseas assignments and the manner in which the criteria were assessed, he noted that the criteria vary from company to company. In general, however, Ohmagari cited the two most important ones as language skills and ability to adapt to a local environment. Although Japanese companies may have no specific mechanism for assessing ability to adapt, because of the strong tradition of groupism in Japanese organizations, the supervisor knows his employees very well. Consequently, he understands the prospective expatriate's strengths and limitations and seldom makes poor decisions in this regard.

When asked why Japanese MNCs use parent-country nationals more extensively than do their U.S. and West European counterparts, he attributed the practice primarily to communication problems between local nationals and Japanese corporate headquarters. In his view, "It is very difficult for foreigners to learn the Japanese language. The Japanese economy as a whole is aggressive, but Japanese people are not aggressive in communicating. It is very difficult for Japanese to communicate with foreigners. We have non-verbal communications; it is implicitly understood." Given the overriding concern for maintaining face, most Japanese tend to approach issues indirectly. Hence, adequate communication with the Japanese entails not only knowledge of the language but also a working understanding of the subtleties associated with it. In the words of a U.S. executive, such communication skills are a "real art" and are rare among the nonnative speakers of the language (Tung 1984b). Despite these difficulties, Japanese MNCs are beginning to use more local nationals at managerial levels in their foreign operations because of host-government requirements and the trend toward establishing manufacturing facilities in foreign countries rather than exporting.

Ohmagari was asked to comment on the role of the family in terms of expatriate assignments. Japanese multinationals have traditionally deemphasized the role of the spouse in the training programs, but the evolving value system of the younger generation might influence that view. According to a survey of one hundred employees of Mitsubishi Electric Co., Ltd., for instance, the increasing reluctance among younger employees to serve abroad stems in part from the spouse's negative opinion (Kawaji 1982). Ohmagari noted that more and more Japanese companies are sponsoring programs for the wives. Indeed, according to a survey conducted by *Japan Economic News* (1982), approximately 30 percent of the responding firms provided seminars for the wives of expatriates prior to departure, either in-house or through external agencies.

Ohmagari noted that there is a general misunderstanding about the role of the family in Japanese society. In reality the family is more important than the company, and wives do play a major role in the family. Japanese husbands are often referred to as "salary men," a designation that stems from a longstanding Japanese tradition that husbands hand their unopened pay envelopes to their wives. In return, their wives give them a daily allowance. However, since "wives are generally not interested in company affairs, they would not interfere" with their husbands' work overseas by complaining about the difficulties of adjusting. A Japanese family's primary concern is the education of the children. According to Ohmagari, "We are a very democratic country—the single most important factor for promotion is education. So people are crazy about education." In Japanese society, a wife's primary responsibility is to her children, and her life revolves around them. Thus, expatriates with children in high school generally leave them in Japan to avoid disrupting their education. In many instances, the wives remain behind to supervise their children's education.

JAPANESE AMERICAN CONVERSATION INSTITUTE (JAPAN)

Another external facility frequently used to prepare candidates for overseas assignments among Japanese MNCs is the Japanese American Conversation Institute (JACI). The information presented here is provided by Namiji Itabashi, chairman of the board of trustees of the International Education Center (IEC), the parent organization of JACI.

History and Objectives

The JACI was established in November 1945 to serve the needs of the Ministry of Finance and other governmental agencies by providing English-language training to young government employees for communicating with the Allied Occupation authorities. As Japan began to expand its international role, the demand for people who could speak fluent English increased. Today the institute serves a much broader audience; its student body is drawn from the financial, business, and government sectors. In addition to language training, the institute offers programs to assist trainees in acquiring a broader understanding of the global arena and to "develop their potential as internationally oriented, well-educated" representatives of Japan (*International Education Center Brochure* 1982). In Itabashi's opinion, the requisites for developing an "international person" are primarily threefold. First, the individual must be a trustworthy and respectable Japanese citizen who can present a good image of Japan to the rest of the world. This person must know Japanese history and culture well because he has to explain his nation to non-Japanese in foreign countries. This criterion echoes the observation made by the *Japan Economic News* (1982) that Japanese expatriates must serve as "roving ambassadors" of Japanese culture. Second, the person must have a "broad, international vision." To promote this objective, the IEC established the School of International Studies (SIS) in 1973, which specializes in international communication, international business, and area studies. Third, the individual must acquire proficiency in at least one foreign language. Since English is the universal language of international business transactions, it should be emphasized. This training is offered by JACI's Scholarship School (Itabashi 1978).

Although the JACI offers other programs, the discussion here centers on the Scholarship School and the SIS. Unlike the IIST, the JACI does not provide dormitory facilities for its trainees. Hence they commute from home.

Scholarship School

The school offers day programs, which meet five hours daily for five days a week, and evening programs, which meet for three hours daily. The day programs range from eleven to twenty weeks; the evening programs last for up to two years.

Itabashi attributes the Japanese schools' emphasis on teaching English through writing to the difficulties many Japanese have in conversing with English-speaking foreigners. He believes that in order to be fluent in a foreign language, trainees need a comprehensive understanding of the foreign culture. In his words, "A language has been developed on the soil of a culture while a culture has been advanced with the language as its blood, and the two are inseparable" (Itabashi 1978: 173). Consequently, the training in both must go hand in hand. Itabashi contends that a good method for improving oral English skills is to help students "think in English." Consequently, a portion of the scholarship school program is devoted to a course entitled "Thinking in English."

This recognition represents a major strength in international development education programs offered by this and other Japanese institutes. In contrast, although some U.S. multinationals may sponsor a crash course in a foreign language for its trainees, it is likely to acquaint the trainees with words and grammar without giving them an adequate understanding of the subtleties and innuendos of the language. Hence, they may unwittingly insult the other party while trying to converse. Chinese and Japanese, for example, are spoken with various levels of formality, depending on whom one is conversing. Consequently, the inappropriate use of certain terminologies, which stems from an inadequate understanding of cultural norms, may do the American expatriate more harm than good.

The program also seeks to teach business negotiating skills and offers courses in listening, note taking, public speaking, debate, and case discussions. At the end of the program, there is a one-week simulation of an international conference, which provides trainees an opportunity to demonstrate their skills in communicating in English and serves as a model for those who have just joined the program (Itabashi 1982).

School of International Studies

The SIS offers a three-month program in international communication, international business, and area studies. The medium of instruction is English, which helps develop the English-language skills of the trainees. Upon completion of the program, trainees are expected to understand the political and cultural environment of the United States, "perform with proficiency and confidence" in a foreign setting, and have a good command of the English language (School of International Studies 1982).

Under this program, over thirty courses in various aspects of international management are taught, mostly by foreign instructors. The areas of study include business negotiations, international finance and accounting, U.S. society and culture, politics, and U.S.-Japan relations. A course that is particularly applicable to international assignments is "Cross-cultural communication," which offers insights into the "day-to-day psychology of human relations"; differentiates between Western and Japanese ways of thinking; and provides hints on "how to handle people (especially foreigners), how to get them to like you (everyone likes to be liked) and how to win people to your way of thinking" (*School of International Studies Brochure* 1982). While its objectives may sound overly ambitious, the very existence of such a course indicates the importance Japanese educational institutes place on human relations skills in doing business abroad.

TRAINING FOR WIVES

The questionnaire survey revealed that a principal factor for failure among expatriates of U.S. and European MNCs is the inability of the family (more particularly, the spouse) to adapt and adjust to a foreign country. When serving overseas, the expatriate spends most of his day in the office and interacts primarily with his coworkers, most of whom speak fluent English and are familiar with American ways. Thus, the expatriate is insulated from the shock and stress of mingling with people who do not understand their language or their culture. The spouse and the children, on the other hand, have greater exposure to members of the local community in their everyday lives. Hence, they are much more susceptible to culture shock.

In contrast, among the sample of Japanese MNCs surveyed, the family situation did not emerge as an important reason for failure. Rather its influence was primarily on the children's education. Although Japanese wives are generally more subservient and, in the words of one Japanese executive, "do not raise much complaints," an increasing number of Japanese corporations are beginning to see the virtues of providing some training to spouses before departure. One reason is that in Japan, wives do not generally engage in the after-hours socializing activities of their husbands, whereas in foreign countries, they are expected to participate in neighborhood and company parties. According to a survey by *Japan Economic News* (1982), approximately 70 percent of the Japanese spouses have greatly increased the amount of time they spend in entertaining, dining out, shopping, working at hobbies, playing sports, and pursuing other leisure activities while overseas. Thus most Japanese wives play a more active role in foreign societies than at home. A wife who is capable of interacting with local nationals will experience less tension and frustration in living overseas. Another reason for providing training is that having a wife who can speak a foreign language and who is at ease in relating to foreigners is an asset to the husband in his career abroad. Therefore several of the Japanese MNCs surveyed have encouraged the wives of expatriates to attend orientation sessions sponsored by outside agencies, such as Japan Air Lines and the Japan Overseas Educational Services (Tung 1984a).

Japan Overseas Educational Services (JOES) was established in 1971 to provide advice and training to the families of Japanese expatriates. JOES is a private, nonprofit organization that receives funding from the Japanese Ministry of Education, the Ministry of Foreign Affairs, and six hundred business entities. It offers a variety of programs, including orientation sessions and consultation programs. The orientation sessions are divided into two categories: environmental briefings and classes on education.

The environmental briefings are offered for the spouses two mornings a week over a two-month period. The briefings are designed to "psychologically prepare" the spouses prior to departure and thus alleviate much of the tension they experience in anticipation of living abroad. According to the survey by the *Japan Economic News* (1982), the average employee departed for a foreign country 4.6 months after notification of the actual overseas assignment. Wives, who generally join their husbands two or three months later, may find the interim waiting period quite stressful.

The environmental briefings are conducted by people who have lived abroad and by people with academic qualifications to address such subjects from both the theoretical and the practical viewpoints. The content of these sessions is primarily factual; they are designed to prepare the wives for daily activities, such as shopping, using public transportation, going to the physician, and so on. The wives also attend lectures on Japanese culture. Given the short duration of the program, language training is minimal; some spouses may supplement it with language courses at other institutes. The focus of the two-month orientation offered by JOES is to provide useful information to the spouses on "how to make oneself understood in the English language" and teach correct pronunciations of the most commonly used English words (Japan Overseas Educational Services 1982).

The orientation program also provides a forum for wives to share their feelings about living abroad and discuss why certain traditional Japanese manners and customs have inhibited them from socializing with non-Japanese. Some of the topics discussed include the Japanese attitude toward religion, the Japanese sense of values, East versus West, hints on dressing, table manners and etiquette, tips on home parties (how to hold parties and how to be invited), and general information on life-styles of foreigners. In 1982 tuition for the two-month program was 50,000 yen and many Japanese multinationals pay such expenses.

The second kind of orientation session is entitled "Preparations for Local Schools in America." Designed for families sent to the United States, it serves a useful function, given the overriding concern with education. This session is divided into parents' and children's classes. In the former, speakers provide information on U.S. schools, both private and public. The speakers have previously taught at weekend schools for Japanese children in the United States—classes held on weekends and designed to familiarize the children of Japanese expatriates with various aspects of Japanese culture—and are versed in providing bilingual education for Japanese youngsters. In the children's classes, experienced trainees use the team approach to reduce participants' anxieties about being educated abroad, even giving tips on how to make friends with American children. The differences between the U.S. and Japanese educational systems, values, and attitudes are also explained. Both classes are offered for three Saturdays every month. In 1982, the tuition for the entire family was 15,000 yen.

In addition to the orientation sessions, JOES provides free consultation to all participants about Japanese weekend schools and the subsequent problems of readjusting to the Japanese school system. This information is made available both prior to departure and on reentry to Japan. Moreover, JOES sends teachers and instructional materials to the Japanese weekend schools for children of expatriates.

A similar, albeit less comprehensive, undertaking in the United Kingdom is the one-day "Living Overseas" program provided by the Women's Corona Society. This facility was used extensively by most of the British multinationals interviewed in this study. The Women's Corona Society is a voluntary association founded in 1950 with the objective of providing assistance, in terms of practical advice and personal contacts, for people going abroad for extended periods of time. The society offers a one-day briefing on living overseas, including such topics as the challenges and rewards of expatriate life as well as health considerations. These briefings are conducted by people who have lived abroad. In addition, there is a consultation session in which the participant may converse, on a one-on-one basis, with someone who has lived in the destination country. In 1984 the cost for the one-day program was 20 pounds. A booklet describing the practical aspects of living abroad was available for an additional 2 pounds.

Although such programs are not comprehensive and do not claim to prepare Japanese and European expatriates' wives for all the contingencies that may arise in living abroad, they are certainly better than nothing. Regrettably, some U.S. multinationals do not provide similar programs for their expatriates.

3 BRITISH MULTINATIONALS

This chapter examines human resource management practices in five British multinationals regarding the staffing of overseas operations and the preparation of British expatriates to promote international commerce. The corporations discussed include two banks, two conglomerates, and the business sector of one of the conglomerates.

These British MNCs represent interesting cases for at least two key reasons. First, until the early twentieth century, the United Kingdom was the most powerful nation in the world, both militarily and economically. Its vast empire spanned the globe, and British civil servants and military personnel occupied positions of authority in many countries worldwide. As such, the Britons have an extensive history of interaction with foreigners, which has given them first-hand knowledge of the dynamics of cross-cultural relationships. Second, Britain's separation from the rest of continental Europe by the British channel has made Britons generally less proficient in foreign languages than their European neighbors. In this regard, the Britons resemble their American counterparts west of the Atlantic. The following examination of the expatriation policies and programs of British MNCs shows both how the expatriates cope with the language issue and how much the knowledge of a foreign language influences successful operations abroad.

BANKS

This section compares the policies and practices at two major U.K. banks: National Westminster Bank (NatWest) and another major bank whose identity is disguised here as the XYZ Bank. Until 1970 NatWest was primarily a U.K. retail bank. Its history of operating overseas is hence very recent. In contrast, XYZ Bank grew out of a merger of three banks that expanded abroad during the heyday of British imperialism more than a century ago. The information presented here was obtained from in-depth interviews with David J. Hurst, assistant personnel manager, and Kay Pierce, an officer at the International Banking Division of NatWest, and two members of management at XYZ Bank. Hurst is responsible for all expatriation and repatriation activities at NatWest. At the time of the interview, he had just completed three and a half years of foreign assignment in the bank's New York office, and thus had also gained personal insight into the bank's expatriation policy.

Overview

The National Westminster Group is one of the world's largest banking groups in terms of capital and reserves. In 1983 it employed 80,665 people in twenty-five countries. Most of its overseas operations are branch or representative offices. Similarly, XYZ is one of the leading banks in the world, with over 5,000 offices in eighty countries. In 1983 it employed a total of 74,988 people.

The International Banking Division at NatWest has grown very rapidly within the past fifteen years. From a zero base in 1970, the division grew to account for 22.1 percent of the group's profits in 1982. In 1983 the International Banking Division employed more than 5,500 people in the United Kingdom and another 5,000 overseas. The majority of its overseas workforce is located in the United States. In 1983, XYZ Bank employed 6,500 people in its International Banking Division in the United Kingdom.

Staffing Policies

Given the recent history of NatWest's international banking activities, the company does not possess a cadre of career expatriates, a common practice among entities that expanded overseas in the nineteenth and early twentieth centuries such as XYZ Bank. The number of expatriate staff at NatWest is low. In 1983 there was only 225 expatriates, 210 of whom were from the United Kingdom. Most are assigned to the world's major financial centers.

In 1983 XYZ Bank had 391 expatriates, excluding third-country nationals and graduate trainees. Due to the policy of localization that accompanied the independence of many countries from British rule, the number of British expatriates has been reduced substantially. About fifteen years ago, for example, XYZ Bank had 120 expatriates in Zambia alone, whereas now that number has dwindled to twenty. Since the bank expanded abroad with the British Empire in the nineteenth century, it has a significant presence in Africa and the Caribbean. The breakdown of geographic location of expatriate staff at XYZ is as follows: 140 in Africa, 70 in North America, 60 in the European Common Market, 36 in East Asia, 20 in the Middle and Near East, 20 in Latin America and the Caribbean, and 37 in Australasia.

At NatWest the duration of an expatriate assignment is from three to five years. Since there are no career expatriates, the assignments abroad are never continuous. In contrast, XYZ Bank has a core of career expatriates. Until two decades ago, these employees spent their careers in given geographic regions moving from one foreign country to another. For example, an expatriate to West Africa would be transferred from Nigeria to Ghana to Sierra Leone. Now, the general policy is for an individual to undertake two postings within a given geographic region. For example, an expatriate to Asia may be assigned to Hong Kong and the Philippines before being sent to another region. The average period of assignment to a given country is from two to three years. In between these assignments, the individual may be stationed in the United Kingdom.

NatWest's expatriates assume a wide variety of positions abroad, ranging from top to middle management positions and nonmanagerial functions. While the company's ultimate objective is to adopt a policy of localization, such a policy is not currently feasible because of the bank's recent entry into overseas activities. No local national has yet acquired adequate knowledge and experience of the group's overall operations to become chief executive officer of a foreign operation. This situation conforms to the theory posited in Chapter 1 that the presence of parent-country nationals is necessary during the start-up phase of an overseas operation. Even in the United States, the country in which NatWest established its first overseas operation, no American employee is yet prepared to head the local bank. Since NatWest is an offshore wholesale bank (rather than a retail bank) that markets its global services to MNCs, the head of a branch operation must be thoroughly familiar with the group's worldwide operations. Only in its minority equity ventures are

NatWest's top-management positions occupied by local nationals. To date, the company has entered into very few such ventures.

NatWest's expatriates are also assigned to nonmanagerial positions, primarily operational and research functions. The reasons for using expatriates in nonmanagerial functions are twofold: one, to ensure that the corporate philosophy and procedures are observed in the offshore centers and two, for career development purposes. Given the growing importance of international banking to the company's overall profits, it is imperative that NatWest develop a cadre of international bankers who have served abroad. Fewer than 20 percent of its expatriates are engaged in nonmanagerial functions.

Recently NatWest has begun to use third-country nationals in its overseas operations. In 1984 fifteen third-country nationals were serving abroad. The decision to hire third-country nationals stems from the bank's ultimate objective to localize foreign operations. Host-country nationals must develop a global perspective and become familiar with NatWest's worldwide operations if they are eventually to manage local subsidiaries. In Hurst's words "We consider it right and proper that (host-country nationals) get this additional experience by undertaking expatriate assignments. That's the general philosophy."

At XYZ Bank expatriates are used only in managerial positions. Until two decades ago, the bank expatriated junior staff who were around twenty-one years of age. It discontinued this practice for three primary reasons. First, the localization requirements of host governments prevented such placement. Second, XYZ's long history of overseas operations has produced indigenous staff who have risen through the ranks of the organizational hierarchy to assume senior positions. In fact, expatriates now no longer monopolize top management positions abroad. In the majority of the bank's foreign operations, both expatriates and host-country nationals occupy managerial positions; the operations in countries such as Canada, France, the Netherlands, New Zealand, and Spain are headed by local nationals. Finally, the high cost of expatriation has served as a major incentive to reduce its use.

At present, third-country nationals account for 8 percent of the total expatriate staff at XYZ Bank. In 1981 the bank established an objective to increase third-country nationals to approximately 20 percent of its expatriate staff. The rationale behind this decision was essentially the same as that at NatWest, namely, to prepare local nationals to take over senior management positions in their respective countries in the future. As XYZ Bank's manager put it, "The idea is generally that we should try to select local staff of high potential so that they can move out, and then move into executive positions in any part of the world.'' A major obstacle to the attainment of this 20-percent target is the cost associated with using third-country nationals. For example, the compensation package paid to maintain the net position at home of a senior level American sent to Nigeria would equal three times the amount paid to a host-country national. Besides exorbitant costs, such assignments also generate problems of inequity.

Selection Criteria and Procedures

NatWest assesses a person's suitability for an overseas position according to four general criteria. The principal criterion is the candidate's competence. Before commencing a search, a job description of the upcoming vacancy is updated to reflect any changes in responsibilities and duties. (Given the rapid expansion of NatWest's international operations, the bank has found it imperative to update the job description each time a vacancy arises.) The candidate's technical qualifications are then matched against the requirements of the position abroad. Given the smaller size of an overseas operation, the expatriate has to undertake a broader range of responsibilities abroad. Thus, the candidate must also possess good administrative skills. Theoretically, the expatriate must show proficiency in the language of the destination country. In practice, however, it may be difficult to find a person who possesses the necessary technical and managerial skills as well as language proficiency, so the language requirement is often compromised. Finally, the candidate must exhibit adaptability and emotional stability. In Hurst's words, the bank seeks someone "who will react well to change, can take increased responsibility, has no medical problems, and has suitable family circumstances.'' The prospective candidate is asked whether there are special circumstances, such as children's education or dependent relatives, that may render an overseas posting inappropriate at the time.

NatWest can generally make an accurate assessment of a person's capabilities along these four criteria because most candidates for managerial expatriate positions have been with the bank for fifteen years at the time of expatriation. Those sent abroad to serve in nonmanagerial functions generally have worked for the bank from five to six years. Since the bank appraises its employees annually on their knowledge, drive, organizational ability, intelligence, ability to communicate, judgment, leadership, personality, and health, it develops a comprehensive profile of each employee, identifying his technical and managerial competence and personality traits, including the family situation.

At NatWest there is generally a twelve-month lead time between the identification of a future vacancy abroad and the actual expatriation. During this period the job requirements are advertised throughout the bank and the respective divisions nominate candidates for the position.

An expatriate candidate can be drawn from either the international or the domestic division of the bank. The selection is made by the career development department, which oversees the career progression and promotion of all staff. After the prospective candidate has been identified, the Service Abroad Section of the International Banking Division interviews him two times. The first interview, held prior to the candidate's appointment to the overseas position, seeks to gauge his interest in the particular position by outlining the responsibilities of the job and explaining the terms and conditions of expatriation, with specific reference to the country of assignment. In addition, the candidate is given an expatriation kit, which contains maps and basic information about the country of assignment, including its cultural environment, educational systems, and so on, along with practical tips for handling an overseas posting, such as how to lease one's property and secure housing abroad, and information on taxation and overseas allowances. The preliminary interview sensitizes the prospective candidate to the negative aspects associated with a particular foreign posting. In Hurst's opinion, "this degree of frankness is in no way counterproductive, as it ensures a durable appointment in the long run." NatWest requests the candidate to discuss the assignment with his family to arrive at "an informed and advised decision" on whether to accept or reject the specific overseas posting, and to inform the bank of his decision within a week. After the Service Abroad Section is convinced that the candidate is suitable, the person will be formally appointed to the position.

At present, the candidate's spouse is not included in the preliminary interview, although recognizing that expatriation is a family affair, NatWest may change that policy. As Pierce observes, "We want it to be a positive experience for the whole family. If one [family member] is unhappy, then the chances are that we will have to bring them back early." However, some candidates resist including their spouses in the selection process, believing that in so doing the bank is prying into family affairs.

After the formal appointment of a candidate for an overseas assignment, there is a second, in-depth interview in which the Service Abroad Section reviews with the appointee a comprehensive checklist covering every conceivable aspect of expatriation. This second interview "builds up the expatriate's confidence in the support he will receive throughout his tour of duty abroad, to take worries off his shoulders, to agree on a timetable of events, and to set in motion a host of practical arrangements," Hurst explained. The bank provides assistance for housing, storage, and transportation of personal effects. The candidate meets with a tax adviser to work out the specific tax implications of the assignment abroad. The candidate and his family then undergo comprehensive medical examinations. In short, the Service Abroad Section of NatWest consciously strives to "achieve . . . a reduction of stress associated with having to get 1,001 things done before they're off," says Hurst.

If a NatWest employee declines an overseas assignment for a valid reason, such as family considerations, it generally does not have an adverse effect upon his candidature for a senior position. However, given the increasing emphasis placed on international operations and the fact that an overseas assignment is considered an integral part of career development, an individual who aspires to top management at NatWest will not repeatedly refuse foreign postings. While the bank accepts that personal considerations may preclude a person from serving abroad at a particular time, it assumes that an aspiring executive will go overseas later, when the impeding circumstances no longer exist. Hurst stated, "We expect that there will be that sort of commitment from our potential senior executive." To support his point, he noted that all members of NatWest's senior management have either served abroad or attended business school overseas. "It is implicit in NatWest, it is known throughout the company, that once a person is selected for an overseas posting, 99 percent of the time it is a promotion. They are keen to make a success in an overseas posting because it is a cue to promotion."

XYZ Bank also uses four criteria for selecting expatriates. Technical competence is paramount. Also, where possible, XYZ Bank tries to find someone who can speak the local language. Since there is a dearth of people with proficiency in exotic languages, this requirement is sometimes relaxed; "much depends on whether or not the language is considered essential to the task to be performed." In addition, the bank looks for adaptability, often manifested by people who have prior experience in living and working abroad. Given its stature in the British financial community and its long history of overseas operations, XYZ can recruit "fairly well-traveled young graduates who know what it is like overseas. Either they are sons and daughters of parents who have been in the diplomatic service, banks, or whatever, or they have done the traveling on their own.'' Furthermore, since XYZ has a cadre of career expatriates, candidates are generally drawn from this pool of people with proven performance records. Finally, the bank considers the individual's potential for senior management. Between 1977 and 1979, the International Banking Division of XYZ Bank conducted an exercise designed to identify the highest level each employee could attain by the time of retirement. Based on this projection, the bank developed the concept of ''career corridors,'' which identify the career progression of an individual at a given time and prescribe the experience the person should obtain at that particular stage. Since international experience constitutes an integral part of career development, an assignment abroad is considered essential for those with good prospects for senior management positions. In the words of XYZ Bank's manager, ''By not being considered for overseas service, the ultimate level that a person could find himself reaching in the organization is lower.'' If a person is assigned overseas within four to six years after joining the bank, he has most likely come through the Management Development Program (described in more detail below). Admission to the program is reserved for those with ''good potential for overseas jobs.'' While XYZ Bank acknowledges that circumstances may prevent a person from accepting an overseas assignment at some point during his career, university graduates who join the International Banking Division are explicitly told, ''If you opt out, you are automatically cutting out two or three jobs that we would like you to have done overseas. Therefore you are not gaining the experience that we would like you to have, and hence it does limit your promotion chances.''

The candidate's spouse is not included in the interview process; rather, the bank relies on the candidate to inform them about the spouse's reservations, if any. Because of its policy of ''cradle-to-grave'' (i.e., lifetime) employment, the bank is generally familiar with the family situations of its employees. According to the manager, ''If a person has a sick wife, we are aware of it. So a picture builds up about the spouse.'' This is similar to the practices in Japanese multinationals (Tung 1984a). At the time of recruitment, XYZ suggests that the employee inform his future spouse about the requirements of the job as it pertains to possible overseas assignments. The bank has very few problems with spouses who cannot adapt to a foreign country. As far as the two managers can recall, there were only one or two such instances.

The selection process is centralized in XYZ Bank's U.K. corporate headquarters. While the regional general managers at headquarters discuss the candidates with the general manager of the foreign subsidiary, the former make the final decision. Since the bank has a cadre of career expatriates, "the personalities being discussed are previously known to both the regional general manager in London, who had him working for him for a different territory before, and the local senior management in the territory knows the individual from previous experience in another part of the world," as one manager explained. Hence, the selection decision is not as autocractic as it might appear. In the event of an overseas job suddenly opening, there is a four-month lead time between the identification of the vacancy and expatriation.

Training Programs

At NatWest the training program consists of the following components: management development, including the acquisition of additional technical skills where necessary; language training; cultural orientation; and contacts with returned expatriates. Each of these components is discussed below.

Management Development Program.   Every year, NatWest recruits from 3,000 to 5,000 people. Most recruits are high school graduates, and some also have university degrees. High school graduates join at the G1 level, while university graduates join at G2 or G3. Above the entry-level positions (G1 through G4), there are the ranks of junior managers or supervisors (A1 through A4). Beyond these are the eight levels of management (M1 through M8). On average, it takes an individual about fifteen years to reach the level of M1.

NatWest provides structured management development programs for its staff, both domestic and international, designed for various stages throughout their careers. These programs are intended to prepare management personnel for every career possibility, including expatriation. They are conducted at either of the bank's two training centers in Oxford and North London. The training center at Oxford can provide residential facilities for 300 trainees.

The person at the M1 level undergoes a two-week residential program entitled "The Role of the Manager." The course helps individuals identify their strengths and limitations and capitalize on the former. It also develops their interpersonal and technical skills. There are from ten to twelve people in a course, but instruction is usually conducted on a one-on-one basis.

Each subsequent level of training continues to develop the person's knowledge and capabilities as a banker. The duration of courses at each level varies but is generally less than two weeks. The mediums of instruction include lectures, case studies, interviews, and videotaped role playing. A person generally completes all in-house management training programs by the M3 level.

NatWest also utilizes outside facilities, such as the one- to two-month executive development programs sponsored by the Manchester Business School (U.K.), the Cranfield School of Management (U.K.), and INSEAD (France).

The Service Abroad Section offers training specific to expatriates. It custom designs two- to three-week programs to familiarize the candidate with each of the departments he may work with while serving abroad. A candidate for an overseas assignment drawn from the domestic banking division undergoes an additional six-week program to learn about international banking activities.

Language Training. For language training, NatWest uses outside facilities such as Berlitz and Lingorama. The bank pays tuition for both the candidate and the spouse. The duration of the language programs varies, ranging from one to two weeks for West European languages to four months for exotic languages such as Japanese. For West European assignments, the bank usually selects a person who already knows the language and merely needs a refresher course.

Cultural Orientation. Candidates assigned to Japan, Saudi Arabia, and South America attend the week-long program offered by the Center for International Briefing, Farnham Castle. At the time of the interview, NatWest was considering having Farnham Castle custom design programs for its expatriates to Hong Kong, Singapore, and Bahrain. For assignees to Japan and Bahrain, NatWest encourages the additional preparation of attending the short courses in language and culture offered by London University's School of Oriental and African Studies. Spouses are encouraged to participate in the "Living Overseas" course sponsored by the Women's Corona Society (described in Chapter 2).

Meetings with Returned Expatriates. Where possible, the candidate and his spouse are encouraged to have lunch or dinner with recently returned expatriates at the bank's expense. Upon arrival in the foreign country, the expatriate and his family are greeted by a reception committee organized by the host center. The host center also generally arranges local accommodations and educational facilities for the new expatriate family and briefs them on practical details such as shopping, driving, and locating a doctor and a dentist.

At XYZ Bank the training program consists of the following components: the Management Development Program, language training, and environmental briefing. Each of these is discussed briefly below.

The Management Development Program (MDP). The MDP was initiated at XYZ Bank in the early 1970s. For each of the two years 1984 and 1985, approximately sixty people were admitted into the MDP. Candidates for the program are drawn from the new recruits with university degrees and the high school graduates who demonstrate potential for managerial positions. As its name implies, the graduates of the program enter into management positions. In 1985, 2 percent of the bank's management personnel have come through the MDP. The bank's objective is eventually to staff 85 percent of its top 750 positions with MDP graduates.

The MDP extends for a full five years, focusing primarily on the acquisition of technical skills. It consists of sequentially planned on-the-job training in the various aspects of the bank's operations interspersed at regular intervals with one- to two-week courses conducted in a classroom setting. An important component of the MDP is an assignment overseas. These foreign postings, required to last a minimum of twelve months, generally run for two years, and, in some cases, may extend to three.

In addition to providing in-house management programs, XYZ Bank also utilizes the facilities at London Business School (U.K.), Harvard University (U.S.A.), Massachusetts Institute of Technology (U.S.A.), and INSEAD (France).

Language Training. At one time, XYZ considered the possibility of "grafting a second language" to every graduate of the MDP, meaning that those who were not proficient in a second language would receive specific language training as part of the program. This proposal has met with opposition in some quarters because of the fear that it will limit a person's career to a given geographic region. There is also concern that the proposal may perpetuate the practice of having career expatriates. The bank is committed to language training, however, and has an in-house facility specifically for the purpose. The present policy is to provide language training after the candidate's destination country has been identified. One of the managers expressed his concern that this practice may in fact carry the same consequences noted above: once a person learns a second language, there is a tendency to send him on future assignments to other countries that speak the same language.

For West European languages, the bank offers refresher courses. In the case of exotic languages, such as Arabic, the candidate undergoes three months of intensive language training at an institute affiliated with the British Foreign Office in Beirut.

Environmental Briefing.   Upon the candidate's request, he and his wife will be sent to the Center for International Briefing, Farnham Castle. In addition, through its long history of overseas operations, XYZ has accumulated a mass of information on foreign countries, which is made available to the expatriates. In special cases, additional training is provided. The person assigned to be the representative of the bank's Beijing (China) office, for example, undertook a year-long program of formal language and cultural studies as well as contacting people who had business dealings with China.

Remuneration Policies

At the time of the interview, the remuneration policy for expatriates at NatWest was under review. In the past, the bank used a build-up approach whereby the home-country salary was treated as the base and adjusted to accommodate the cost-of-living differential, the tax differential, and foreign exchange fluctuations. In this way, the expatriate could not experience a decrease in his standard of living while abroad.

According to Hurst, NatWest was contemplating adopting a balance sheet approach instead. Under this method, the spendable portion of the expatriate's income would be inflated for the cost-of-living differential, while the savings portion would be protected from exchange rate fluctuations.

To provide an incentive to work overseas, at the time of the assignment, an expatriation allowance of 550 pounds is given to married couples and 325 pounds to single people. If the children remain in England for schooling, the bank pays their boarding school expenses plus three roundtrip airfares between Britain and the foreign country annually. For assignments to less desirable locations, an additional hardship premium is paid.

Similar to NatWest, the philosophy at XYZ Bank is that an expatriate should enjoy at least the same standard of living abroad as he has domestically. Thus its compensation package takes into account the following: the cost-of-living differential in the foreign country, punitive taxation, local equivalent salary (i.e., the expatriate will earn at least the same salary as that paid for comparable positions in the destination country), the level of commitment at home (such as children in domestic boarding schools and retaining a residence there), a hardship premium, and an inducement factor. The latter is determined by the region of assignment and the expatriate's level of seniority. At one time, the bank provided free furnished accommodations to all expatriates. Now, however, the expatriate pays a portion of the rent, which sum is not to exceed 10 percent of his local salary. As an incentive to serve abroad, the expatriate is usually provided accommodations superior to those he can afford at home. In general, the more senior the person and the more difficult the foreign conditions, the higher the quality of accommodations. In the past, when XYZ Bank deployed a large number of expatriates, there was an established scale of overseas compensation pegged to the person's base salary at home. Since the number of expatriates has been reduced substantially, such set scales have been eliminated. The compensation package is now arranged for each individual case.

The policy of adjusting the expatriate's compensation to match salaries for equivalent positions in the host nation sometimes poses problems in countries such as the United States. Given the substantially higher salary structure in the United States, some expatriates may be reluctant to take reductions in their salaries by returning to the United Kingdom. Furthermore, given the bank's very rapid expansion in the United States, these expatriates have acquired expertise and experience invaluable to the bank's operations there. This poses a dilemma for corporate headquarters. Due to the size and significance of the U.S. operation, generally those with the highest potential are assigned to work there. However, the pragmatics of the situation may prompt some of those valuable expatriates to want to remain in America. Although XYZ Bank is reluctant to lose these people to its U.S. operation, it is faced with the alternative of losing them altogether to another American employer. Consequently, the bank usually allows these expatriates to become permanent assignees. Once this happens, however, they lose all expatriate benefits and become subject to local terms of employment. NatWest is confronted with a similar situation. In the past four years, two of its expatriates to the United States have opted for local terms.

Repatriation

Increasingly, multinationals find that repatriation may be an equally traumatic experience as expatriation because of problems of reabsorption, both professionally and personally. To facilitate the transfer home, NatWest provides a repatriation package modeled after the expatriation kit. Six months prior to repatriation, the Service Abroad Section informs the expatriate of his next assignment and sends him a repatriation checklist package, containing customs declaration forms and other information about the transfer home. A repatriation allowance of approximately 1,500 pounds is also paid to smooth the transition.

A major concern of American expatriates about long overseas assignments is that prolonged absence from corporate headquarters may inhibit their subsequent career advancement within the organization. Hurst indicated that this was not the case at NatWest for three reasons. One, an overseas posting is generally recognized as a cue for promotion. Two, the typical assignment abroad is short, and in most cases, expatriates do not take on consecutive overseas assignments. Only two people have served abroad for longer than seven years. According to Hurst, "An overseas assignment is a short phase in one's career." Finally, for career development purposes, the expatriate remains within the jurisdiction of corporate headquarters while abroad. Hence, an expatriate's career aspirations would not be neglected while he is overseas.

The managers at XYZ Bank acknowledged that repatriation may pose a problem among career expatriates. Foreign countries' localization policies are necessitating the repatriation of many career expatriates. A number of these returnees are in their late forties yet are capable only of filling relatively junior management positions at home. While retraining is feasible for the younger returnees, it is much more difficult for the older ones. One of XYZ's managers admitted that "it is very difficult to redeploy those people. . . . One cannot deny that a good number of people are, at the moment, in supernumerary positions, simply awaiting replacement." To alleviate the situation, the bank offers the option of early retirement to those over age fifty. People who have served in less desirable locations can accumulate "declared area service" points, which grant them three months toward retirement for every year of service in these countries. They are allowed to accumulate a maximum of five years off from the regular retirement age of sixty.

When asked whether the difficulty of properly placing returnees may deter young aspiring talents from serving abroad, the manager at XYZ Bank admitted that some people may indeed feel threatened. However, he contended that this unfortunate situation was a legacy of the past practice of permanent expatriation, a policy that is now being phased out. Once the existing pool of career expatriates has retired, the placement issue will be moot. The new generation of expatriates at the management level serves on two- to three-year stints, and the duration of overseas assignment for management trainees is just twelve months.

Success and Reasons for Success

The rate of expatriate failure at NatWest is quite low: between 2 and 3 percent. The cases of failure can generally be ascribed to health reasons, domestic problems, and lack of business skills, both technical and relational. If the failure occurs because of health reasons or factors beyond the control of the expatriate, it generally does not have an adverse effect on his subsequent career advancement.

At XYZ Bank the incidence of expatriate failure is less than 1 percent. These rare occurrences are most often attributed to domestic problems. Inability to complete one's tour of duty abroad does have a negative impact upon the person's advancement at XYZ. In the case of one expatriate who returned almost immediately because he disliked the foreign country, "there was quite an inquest held," and he was demoted. Although he later requested to be expatriated again, the bank denied his request. Since overseas experience is considered an essential step in career development, this person's chances of advancement are clearly limited by his lack of overseas service. In another instance, an expatriate requested early return because he was held up at gunpoint in the foreign country. According to one manager, the bank's attitude was that "he should not be allowed to benefit" from the situation by being transferred home prematurely, "although people were sympathetic of the reasons why he asked to come out." The individual adjusted to the situation in due time and remained in the foreign country for his full tour of duty.

Three common factors emerge as key to the success in expatriation at NatWest and XYZ Bank. The first is the importance attached to international assignments. At both banks, an international assignment is considered an essential step in career development and is generally recognized as a cue for promotion. Moreover, there is a longstanding tradition of internationalism in the United Kingdom. According to one manager at XYZ Bank, "Everything, every war that we had to fight, has always meant that we have to leave the shores." Given Britain's intrinsic international orientation (the country exports one-third of its GNP) many British have an expressed desire to work overseas. Most families, in fact, have at least one member who has worked, or is currently living, abroad. Another manager at XYZ Bank observes that this may be a legacy of the "Empire spirit. People join organizations like ours and the Foreign Service simply because they want to work overseas." Even for those recruited into the domestic banking division, where the chances of expatriation are very remote, "there is always the hope that perhaps at the end of the day, somebody is going to ask them to go overseas for a period."

Second is the support system designed to allay expatriates' concerns about repatriation. Although an overseas assignment locates the employee far from the mainstream of corporate headquarters, the chances that he will be bypassed for promotion are minimal. NatWest has established sponsorship program to update the expatriate's records in London. During each annual vacation home, the expatriate is requested to discuss career plans with headquarters, and during the last home leave, he is required to meet with the Career Development Department. According to Pierce, the expatriates "actually feel that we do care for them." As noted earlier, returnees are also given a comprehensive repatriation kit to smooth their transition home. Similarly, the career planning section of XYZ Bank's personnel division discusses career goals with the expatriate during every home leave. In these meetings the expatriate is "given an indication of what his future is like."

The third component is the quality of the people sent abroad. Both banks select their top employees for international assignments to further their career development. In fact, XYZ Bank believes that its expatriates are overqualified for some foreign assignments.

Other reasons for the high success rates at NatWest are the short duration of overseas assignment, the provision of comprehensive preparatory programs and the desirable locations of most assignments. As previously noted, most assignments are to major financial centers of the world. These offices are well established, so the "expatriates are not breaking any frontier," to quote Hurst.

Additional reasons for XYZ Bank's success include its cadre of career expatriates and its tolerant attitude toward less-than-average performance abroad during the initial period of assignment. In the words of one manager, "We are slightly more tolerant. There is far less of a 'hire and fire' attitude. There are people who don't get wonderful reports.'' These individuals are allowed to complete their tour of duty but may not be sent overseas again. The number of people in this category is minimal, however.

Proposed Changes

Both NatWest and XYZ Bank were asked to comment on possible changes to their present expatriation policies. NatWest, as noted earlier, is contemplating conversion to a balance sheet approach in their remuneration for overseas service. Hurst also expressed a desire to place greater emphasis on linguistic abilities because of the bank's growing international involvement. He believes the bank is taking measures to develop a ''truly multilingual cadre of bankers for the future.''

Managers at XYZ Bank hope that once the career expatriates have been phased out, overseas assignments can be used primarily for career development purposes, not merely to fill vacancies. This will overcome the problem of redeployment of repatriatees. XYZ's Management Development Program is intended to accomplish this objective. A second proposed change is to utilize more fully the talent of the indigenous staff. The bank has identified local nationals with high potential and is currently grooming them for higher level positions in the future. In fact, 70 to 75 percent of the participants in the intermediate management programs held in London are now non-Britons. ''We make sure that their potential is confirmed by the general management in London, in terms of developing their career internationally rather than locally.'' A third area of proposed changes is to improve the linguistic skills of the graduates of the Management Development Program.

CONGLOMERATES

This section examines the policies and practices at two British conglomerates, Imperial Chemical Industries P.L.C. (ICI) and British Petroleum Company P.L.C. (BP). In addition, the practice at one of BP's twelve business sectors will be discussed. This sector, having chosen to disguise its identity, will be referred to as BPx International. An examination of its policies will shed light on the extent to which separate business entities of a conglomerate are centralized or decentralized. According to the manager of BPx International, in general, their staffing policies are not widely divergent because "we have a lot of connections—we support them and they us."

The information on ICI was obtained from in-depth interviews with Peter H. Rogers, manager of the International Personnel Group, and David Wootton, another member of management of the Personnel Group. Rogers is an Australian national on assignment to the United Kingdom. The information on BP and BPx International was obtained from Roger J. Austin, management development adviser, and two managers from one of the group's business sectors.

Overview

ICI was established in 1926. Today, it is one of the largest chemical groups in the world, with nine business sectors: petrochemicals and plastics; oil; general chemicals; agriculture; pharmaceuticals; paint; fibers; industrial explosives; and colors, polyurethane, and specialty chemicals. The group has operations in 140 countries and manufacturing facilities in 60. The majority of its overseas subsidiaries are wholly or majority owned. Increasingly, the company is expanding through acquisitions. In acquisitions, ICI prefers to leave the personnel policy and practices of the acquired company intact; thus expatriates are seldom, if ever, used in companies that are acquired. In 1983, the group employed 117,900 people, 61,800 of whom were located in the United Kingdom. Group sales in 1983 were 8,256 million pounds, 50 percent of which were derived from West Europe (29 percent from the United Kingdom and 21 percent from continental West Europe), 22 percent from the Americas, 18 percent from the Far East and Australasia, and 10 percent from other countries.

BP was established in 1909. For the first twenty-five years, its operations were confined to the development, production, and sales of Iranian oil. Since then, the company has diversified considerably to include twelve business sectors: BP Exploration, BP Oil International, BP Chemicals International, BP Minerals International, BP Coal, BP Gas, BP Detergents International, BP Ventures, BP Shipping, BP Nutrition, Scicon International (an information technology industry), and Sohio (a diversified energy and natural resources group based in Cleveland, Ohio, in which BP has a 53 percent equity interest). The group employs 132,000 people, 33,000 of whom are located in the United Kingdom. BP has 1,900 subsidiaries and related businesses in some seventy countries. The BP Group is organized on a three-dimensional matrix structure: region, business, and function.

Staffing Policies

The history of expatriation at ICI and BP dates back to the companies' formation in 1926 and 1909, respectively. Like those of other British MNCs, ICI's expatriate staff has declined substantially in number over the past two decades; its present level is 550 people, including third-country nationals. This cutback stems from ICI's policy to use indigenous people, where possible. Effective localization requires recruiting and retaining high-calibre local nationals to work for ICI, which might be difficult if all senior positions were monopolized by Britons. In addition, the high cost of expatriation and the localization policies of host governments, which render it difficult for foreign nationals to obtain work permits, encourage ICI to employ nationals.

Most of the 550 transferees are assigned to the United States and Western Europe. ICI's operations in the Middle East, with the exceptions of those in Turkey and Israel, are limited in scale. Most are small commercial offices engaged in trading functions only. Of the 550 transferees, approximately 250 are third-country nationals.

In general, ICI's international assignments can be classified into three categories. Technical assignments occur at the lower levels of management and are undertaken primarily for the transfer of technology and skills to an overseas subsidiary. Transfers in this category generally involve sending host-country nationals to the United Kingdom or elsewhere to acquire new technical skills. Approximately 55 percent of international transferees fall into this category. Career development rotations generally occur at the middle management level. In the mid-1970s, the ICI board of directors established an objective of having at least one-third of the company's top management personnel possess significant overseas experience by the next decade. Although the goal had not been met by 1984, the board reaffirmed it. Sending employees with high potential on short stints abroad will ensure that future members of senior management will have international experience. Senior management level appointments are made when the foreign subsidiary lacks appropriate nationals to head its operations. About 10 percent of the expatriate assignments fall into this category.

The stage of development of a foreign operation may not necessarily correlate with the level of overall economic development attained in that country. For example, while Japan is an industrialized country, ICI's top man there is a Briton. ICI established operations in Japan in the 1930s, but they were disrupted during World War II. Consequently, at present no Japanese national has been with the company long enough to have developed the necessary contacts with the U.K. parent organization and elsewhere to successfully head the local operation. Wootton believes that this situation will eventually change since Japanese nationals are now being groomed for senior management positions. To ameliorate the obvious difficulties involved with a non-Japanese supervisor relating to Japanese employees, the local personnel director is a Japanese national. The Japanese personnel director interfaces with people internally, while the British CEO liaises with the U.K. parent organization and other foreign operations. In contrast, the ICI subsidiaries in India and Pakistan are headed by local nationals. This can be attributed to the long history of ICI's operations in these countries.

The duration of assignments for the first two categories of international transfers (i.e., technical positions and career development rotations) is from two to three years. Appointments at the senior executive level average from ten to fifteen years. In some cases, they may become permanent assignments, and the person moves from one senior position to another more senior posting elsewhere in the world. The number of permanent expatriates is low—at present, there are only twenty permanent expatriates, six of whom are stationed outside of continental Western Europe.

BP's expatriate staff is larger than that at ICI. The BP Group has 1,344 British expatriates and 150 international transferees to the United Kingdom. Like most multinationals, BP has decreased its use of expatriates over the past two decades for two primary reasons: the parent company's desire to grant greater autonomy to its local subsidiaries and the localization policies of host governments.

At BP most expatriates are engaged in exploration and production functions in the developing countries. For offshore exploration projects, the staff is almost exclusively expatriate, with Britons occupying technical positions and Indians and Pakistanis engaged as laborers. The heavy use of expatriate staff in the Gulf States stems from the small populations in the region and the reluctance of the indigenous people to work offshore. Educated local nationals prefer supervisory and managerial positions onshore. Some of the Britons assigned to the Middle East are permanent expatriates. One contingent, for example, has worked in Abu Dadi for over twenty years.

In general, BP's overseas staffing policy is determined by three major considerations: the host-country's requirements, the size of the overseas operation, and the desire to staff positions with the best available people. The first consideration, being self-explanatory, will not be elaborated upon.

With regard to size, the top management personnel of large associate companies are usually host-country nationals, while British nationals head the small ones. The size of an associate company is determined by its revenue, assets, staff, and functions performed. The large subsidiaries engage in marketing, may operate refining facilities, and may engage in several businesses, such as chemicals and nutrition. BP's four largest subsidiaries—Sohio (in the United States), BP Australia, BP France, and BP Germany—are all headed by host-country nationals. British expatriates may occupy middle management positions, primarily for career development purposes. Assignments at this level are generally done on an exchange basis. The small subsidiaries, in comparison, engage in marketing functions only and are generally headed by Britons.

The second consideration, the size of the overseas operation, may be superseded by the third factor, namely, the desire to staff the position with the best available person. For example, when the present Australian chief executive retires, he will most probably be replaced by a British national "because it is believed that none of the present Australian directors have the capability to actually take over the job." Moreover, as a big multibusiness operation, the Australian branch is a good training ground to prepare executives who may eventually be promoted to the main board in the United Kingdom. Conversely, the small associate company located in Belgium is headed by a Belgian because he is the best person for the job, all things considered.

Austin described the BP group structure as pyramidal. At the lower levels of management, staffing functions are decentralized. Toward the top of the pyramid, however, "people stop [being] the property of their local company or their functional departments in London. They are seen as a group resource." At this level, the objective is to staff the position with the best available person, regardless of his country of origin. All appointments at the senior management level must be ratified by the Senior Management Committee in London. Therefore, local appointments to senior positions may be overruled at times. Generally, however, the large associate companies enjoy a fair amount of autonomy in making appointments. In the case of Sohio, for instance, aside from sending some nominated board members from the United Kingdom, BP does not interfere in any way with the management of the operation. When British expatriates are stationed in the United States, they are done solely on an exchange basis. The autonomous operation of the large associate companies may, of course, complicate the international rotation of staff for career development purposes.

According to Austin, the BP group seeks to move toward a truly global staffing orientation. In his words, "To call us multinational is a little bit misleading. We are actually a British international company." At present, the mobility of third-country nationals is fairly restricted. There are currently fewer than twenty-four third-country nationals, and most of the international assignments are transfers to and from the United Kingdom. BP's current board wants to rectify this situation by ensuring that indigenous employees with high potential, particularly those from the small associate companies, can be "identified and recognized as a group resource rather than just a local country resource." As part of their career development, it is imperative to increase their international mobility. There are problems associated with the implementation of this policy, however. Once the local nationals of the small associate companies acquire experience in third countries, they may outgrow the scope of their own country's operation. At that stage, they must choose whether to become permanent expatriates. This is not an easy decision.

At BP the average duration of an overseas assignment is from two to three years. Exploration projects that yield only dry holes may be abandoned in six to nine months and the people recalled home.

Selection Criteria and Procedures

At ICI the selection criteria and procedures vary according to the three categories of overseas assignments. For positions involving the transfer of technical skills, the selection decision is made primarily between the subsidiary that can supply the individual and the operation that needs him. The International Personnel Group is involved only in finalizing the arrangements for the transfer. The spouse's adaptability is not taken into consideration because she may not accompany the husband abroad. For assignments to Saudi Arabia, for example, the wife usually remains at home. When the family remains behind, the expatriate is entitled to more frequent trips home based on the total number of flights that would have been taken if his wife and children had gone along. He is granted the same number of flights to return home or to fly the family abroad during holidays.

In selecting candidates for overseas assignments for career development purposes, the principal criterion is whether a person has potential for senior management positions. Candidates for this category are drawn from the pool of high achievers, as assessed by ICI's high-achiever program. The company then evaluates the person's work record, language capability, and flexibility in a new environment. To gauge the latter dimension, the International Personnel Group is collaborating with British academic circles in developing a psychometric test of adaptability to foreign environments.

For senior management positions, an announcement describing the vacancy and requirements for filling it is circulated around the company worldwide. Nominations are then submitted by potential candidates, a short list of prospective candidates is generated, and the top-ranking candidates are then interviewed. While the criteria vary according to the specific position, in general, the most important attributes are (1) technical competence (in Rogers' words, "Knowledge of the right product range is primary"); (2) adaptability to a foreign country, including the family situation; and (3) previous international work experience, a desirable but not absolutely essential requirement.

In general, knowledge of the foreign language is not crucial. ICI's preference is to find a person with the appropriate technical skills and then send him to intensive language training, rather than recruiting one who has linguistic skills but is deficient in the technical aspect. The spouse's suitability for the foreign posting is gauged through social interactions, rather than in an inteview. For appointments at the most senior level, the candidate and spouse are sent to the destination country to get a first-hand impression of the environment and to meet with members of top management there. According to Rogers, people are often eliminated from serious consideration because of inappropriate family circumstances.

ICI concedes that dual-career families pose a serious problem, although there are still few such families at this time. In transfers within the United Kingdom, ICI's policy has been to reimburse the wife for up to six months of lost earnings, provided she is actively seeking a suitable position in the new location. For families in which the spouse is not a professional, the financial package provided by ICI may constitute a sufficient incentive. In cases where the spouse is a professional, however, it cannot adequately compensate the family for lost career opportunities. Consequently, prospective candidates may opt out of a foreign posting. In international assignments, the career problem is more complicated because some countries, such as Australia, will not grant a work permit to the spouse of an expatriate.

If an individual refuses an overseas assignment for valid family reasons, generally, "it is not some big stain that will thwart his movement in the future," said Wootton. The company realizes that people may not be mobile at certain stages in their lives. However, if an employee repeatedly refuses an overseas assignment, given ICI's extensive operations world-wide and the board's commitment to providing international experience to at least a third of its senior management personnel, it may limit the level to which the person can rise because he has "less valid experience than somebody else," to quote Wootton. This is similar to the observation made by a manager of XYZ Bank.

In the case of BP, four primary criteria are used to select people for overseas assignments. Technical competence is first and foremost. Language proficiency is particularly important in assignments to West European countries. Adaptability to new environmental settings is an important consideration in postings to senior management positions in the Far East and the Middle East. In the case of BP's latest venture in China, a key attribute required of the candidate was patience. Given the culture, political system, and business practices in China, matters do not progress as rapidly as in the West. Since the senior manager assigned there has frequent dealings with the Chinese government, he "has to be a diplomat as well as a technical expert." As noted earlier, the majority of assignments at BP are in exploration and production functions. For assignments in these categories, the adaptability criterion is not a major consideration because these jobs are primarily "introverted roles in the company," requiring minimal interaction with members of the local community. Finally, the candidate's potential for a senior management position is considered. Like XYZ Bank and ICI, BP assesses all of its managers regarding the ultimate level they can be expected to reach in the organizational hierarchy. If a candidate's projected level is below grade 14, that is below the level of general manager, the company will not expatriate him for two interrelated reasons. First, the sheer cost of expatriation prompts the company to reserve the opportunity for those with high potential for attaining senior management positions. According to the manager of BPx International, they "really want to give that experience only to the best people we have." Second, to capitalize on its corporate resources, the company wants to place the repatriate in a suitable position that will utilize his overseas experience. According to a manager at BPx International, "If you send somebody abroad who can do the job but whom we reckon does not have any more potential for advancement upon return, he will be harder to reabsorb. . . . We actually like to see it as an experience or a stage in a career that will blossom afterwards."

Candidates for an overseas posting are requested to discuss the assignment with their spouses. In addition, the spouses are given an opportunity to discuss living and working conditions in the destination country with people from the Central Postings Group. Matters such as the country's attitude toward women are approached "openly and in an upfront manner, and they can be a feature for a negative decision on the matter," to quote Austin. In reviewing the company's experiences, he noted that BP has few problems with the family situation except in the Middle East, where the divorce rate among expatriates is higher than that in other parts of the world. In assignments to the Middle East where the family remains behind in the United Kingdom, expatriates are given very generous home leaves. For example, a person on a three-year assignment can take an annual two- to three-month home leave. Since expatriates in those locations work long hours, even with such extensive home leaves, they put in the same number of work hours per annum as do their British counterparts.

As in the case of ICI, if a BP employee declines an overseas assignment for a valid reason, such as children's education or a working spouse, it generally does not have an adverse effect upon his or her subsequent advancement. In the past two decades, BP has adopted a more liberal attitude toward lack of mobility among its employees at certain stages in their careers. In fact, in the annual assessments, employees are specifically asked whether there are any constraints on their mobility. In the past, according to Austin, "it was like joining the Foreign Service where everybody is expected to pack his bags and be off on a plane in a week. If you had problems, you left your wife behind." If a person declines an overseas posting because of sheer parochialism, that is, if the family simply does not want to leave the United Kingdom, the matter is discussed in the context of possible constraints on the employee's career progression, "not as a sort of negative black mark, but more as a practical point that it is the right developmental job for you and it happens to be overseas, and you turned it down, so there is always a possibility that a similar job may not occur again in the same time frame, and therefore promotion may be slower." Like NatWest, BP expects an extra degree of commitment from its small cadre of high achievers.

The candidate for an overseas assignment is selected jointly by the associate company that has the vacancy and the functional or business unit in the United Kingdom that can fill the need. The personnel division gives advice to line management and helps them prepare a short list of candidates. The final selection, however, is the prerogative of line management.

Training Programs

The training programs at ICI can be categorized into the following: technical and management training, cross-cultural briefing, and language training. Each of these is discussed briefly below.

Technical and Management Training.   All levels of managers receive technical and management training. Programs at the junior management level are decentralized and are sponsored by the respective subsidiaries. At the middle management level, management programs are centralized. Foreign nationals attend group-wide programs at ICI's training center in Cranfield, sometimes followed by on-the-job training in headquarters, in which case it may extend for three years. At the time of the interview, for example, one of ICI's Japanese employees had just completed a one-year program at Cranfield and was about to be assigned to one of the group's divisions for two years and then repatriated to ICI (Japan) Ltd. At the senior management level, people may attend external programs such as Harvard Business School's eleven-week Advanced Management Program.

Cross-cultural Briefing.   This is provided in-house. Each expatriate is given a packet containing literature prepared by Employment Conditions Abroad Ltd. addressing the socio-cultural, political, and economic situations in the destination country. In addition, it provides information on immigration rules, remittance of funds, overseas schools, banks, and so on. ICI expects the expatriate to engage in further research in public libraries and elsewhere to learn as much as possible about the foreign country. According to Wootton, "We are not in the business of spoon-feeding every single person who is going abroad as if he were totally incapable of doing things for himself."

In appropriate situations, the candidate and his spouse attend the week-long program at the Center for International Briefing, Farnham Castle. At present ICI sends only a relatively small number of people, about fifty expatriates, to Farnham annually. The programs may not be offered at the time to coincide with expatriation, since there is usually a six-month lead time for expatriates in technical positions and career development rotation assignments. For assignments at the senior management level, however, the lead time may be as long as twelve months. Also, the International Personnel Group feels that the program "covers more than what our needs might be.'' Since Farnham's programs are organized on a regional basis, an expatriate to Indonesia also learns about Malaysia, Thailand, and Burma. This is deemed useful for senior management personnel but superfluous for assignees at junior levels. Wootton observed that ''Farnham Castle does not particularly care whether [trainees are] junior or more senior people.''

As part of the preparation for appointments at the senior management level, the expatriate and his wife are actually sent to the country of assignment to facilitate cultural adaptation. At the lower levels of management, where possible, the company arranges for the outgoing family to meet with the returning family for a briefing on the situation in the destination country. In addition, upon arrival in the foreign country, the wives of other ICI expatriates offer assistance to help the newcomers settle in as quickly as possible.

Language Training.   Since English is the *lingua franca* of international business transactions, Wootton observed that ''there seems to be less pressure on the Britons to learn other languages.'' In the majority of cases, expatriates are simply provided with language tapes to learn at their own pace. There are exceptions, however. For example, the person assigned to head the Japanese operation studied Japanese for three weeks at the Institute of Oriental Studies at London University and continued further private language lessons after arriving in Japan.

At BP training programs fall into the categories of management training, environmental briefing, and language training.

Management Training.   Management training programs are classified into Stages 1, 2, and 3. A university graduate generally joins BP at Grade 8 (or 400 Hay points). At that level, Stage 1 training is provided. This is a week-long program that exposes recruits to the nature of the group's operations. At the middle management level (around 650 Hay points), the employee is introduced to the Stage 2 program. The purpose of this two-week residential course, held at BP's Management Training Center outside of London, is to examine environmental constraints on BP's operations and to allow managers and senior specialists an opportunity to discuss corporate and regional strategies for meeting domestic and worldwide challenges. The Stage 3 program is provided for senior management personnel (grade 13 or 1,000 Hay points). It is a two-week residential course to provide a forum for members of senior management from around the globe to discuss strategies at corporate headquarters and the associate companies.

Employees showing high potential also attend seminars and one-year MBA programs sponsored by external agencies. Members of senior management may attend executive education programs offered by Harvard and Stanford universities.

Environmental Briefing.   This type of instruction is offered through the Central Postings Group at the head office, which has responsibility for international transfers. During BP's long history of overseas operation, it has accumulated extensive information about many countries. In addition, the dozen or so staff members of the Central Postings Group visit the overseas subsidiaries at regular intervals and meet with repatriates. Consequently, they possess up-to-date knowledge about host societies.

The expatriate and his wife meet with staff members of the Central Postings Group for sixty to ninety minutes to discuss various aspects of living and working in the destination country, such as local customs and clothing. Candidates for assignments to exotic countries attend the week-long program offered by Farnham Castle.

According to one manager, BPx International's expatriates are always sent to established centers abroad. In China, for example, there are already one hundred expatriate families, and in Indonesia, from twenty to thirty families. Austin noted that BP expatriates tend to "congregate in colonies wherever we go." This appears to be a common practice among British expatriates. The wives of expatriates organize local company clubs that undertake much of the responsibility of acculturating the newcomers. Thus, "there is already considerable expertise in the country to get the people sorted out." In the Geneva operation, for example, where there are two hundred employees, there is a full-time personnel officer whose sole responsibility is to take care of the needs of expatriates, including renting houses and providing advice on schools, shopping, and so on. Like ICI, BP is a member of the Employment Conditions Abroad Ltd. and subscribes to its services, one of which is to provide information to BP employees.

Virtually no training is provided for the exploration staff because these people "have committed themselves to a lifetime of working in overseas locations. They and their families would expect it. It is not really a problem," explained a BPx manager.

Language Programs.   To facilitate the acquisition of linguistic skills, BP uses outside facilities such as Berlitz. The duration of the program depends on the person's proficiency in the language and the nature of the assignment abroad. If the person already has a high-school knowledge- (about five years of instruction) of the foreign language, he needs only a two- to three-week refresher course. For senior level appointments to exotic locations, the duration of the language training is generally six weeks, followed by further tutoring upon arrival in the destination country. The exploration staff are taught the basics of the language to enable them to hire taxis and order meals in the foreign location.

BP encourages the spouses of expatriates to take language training and provides them with language tapes and facilities for listening to them. Further training is generally made available to the wives upon their arrival in the foreign country. "One way to overcome some of the culture shock of adaptation for the spouse," observed Austin, "is to be busy in the first couple of months. A way to keep busy is to go off and learn the language."

Remuneration Policies

ICI reviews the statistics of essential spending in various foreign countries prepared by Employment Conditions Abroad Ltd. and the Organization Resources Council and compensates expatriates according to the cost-of-living adjustment indices issued by these two agencies. In addition, the company incorporates its expatriates' residual expenses, such as for children remaining in boarding school or for retaining a home in Britain, into the compensation package. Wootton explained, "In general, we try to meet all the expenses involved in the normal lifestyle and those additional expenses that arise because we have sent them overseas." For example, as a matter of common practice, expatriates to Malaysia have household servants. Consequently, their compensation packages include a provision for servants.

The overseas incentive at ICI amounts to approximately ten percent of the employee's gross salary. For assignments to hardship locations, ICI uses a system developed by Employment Conditions Abroad Ltd. that assesses a country along ten dimensions: distance from home; ease or difficulty of getting to and from the United Kingdom; climate; ease or difficulty of acquiring facility in the local language; health considerations; quality of health care facilities; availability of English-language schools; quality of education; availability of goods, services, and recreational facilities; and risks to personal and family well-being such as terrorism and robbery. Based on these factors, countries are categorized into five major groups. At one end are countries like Canada, the United States, and

Australia. At the other extreme are countries such as Bangladesh, Nigeria, Guatamala, and Honduras. The more difficult the local conditions abroad, the higher the hardship premium. To make assignments to hardship locations more palatable, the compensation may not merely be in the form of money but also in improved living conditions. For example, expatriates assigned to ICI's soda-ash plant in the deserts of Kenya are entitled to recreational trips to Mombasa, a seaside resort, once every six to eight weeks. For assignments to all hardship locations, the expatriate family is entitled to two annual home leaves instead of the usual one.

Expatriates assigned to the United States are paid a local salary. Given the strong dollar at the time of the interview, Wootton indicated that "the normal pay would almost be sufficient in itself to provide an incentive and a high standard of living." When asked whether the high U.S. salaries may lead some British expatriates to go native, as had happened at NatWest and XYZ Bank, he indicated that such occurrences are rare. Most people simply regard 'the period overseas with higher pay and savings potential as a 'windfall' situation.''

The renumeration policy at BP is essentially the same as ICI: the expatriate is compensated for the cost-of-living differential and is given a foreign allowance and a hardship premium for postings to difficult locations. According to a manager at BPx International, in 1984, the average cost of expatriating a family was 100,000 pounds. If the base compensation in London was 100 points, the same position in Geneva would be indexed at 200 points.

Repatriation

In 1983 ICI had 117,900 employees, down from 123,800 in 1982. Rogers acknowledged that this decrease in the total number of employees may cause some repatriation problems. ICI guarantees each returning employee reentry into the organizational unit that expatriated him, but Wootton contended that the right job for the returnee may not always coincide with the date of repatriation. "So for six months or more, the repatriate may just fill a job that is manufactured or put together so that he has something to do. But that is just a holding situation while his home country is finding a better place to use the experience he has gained."

BP has a parentage system for monitoring the career path of its expatriates. Under this system each expatriate is assigned a mentor at home and a senior manager abroad who is responsible for his well-being while overseas. According to Austin, "Everybody has a parent (usually a member of senior management) who is looking after his interest and career development back in the United Kingdom." The mentor has the responsibility to keep abreast of what the expatriate is learning in the overseas position and, once every six months, to discuss with him career objectives upon repatriation. This practice is similar to the support mechanism provided by many Japanese MNCs (Tung 1984a). Since the job turnover at the senior management level is virtually nonexistent, when the mentor moves to a new position within the company, he takes the sponsorship with him. In the words of a manager at BPx International, "The personal link is the vital thing, not the link by way of what role the general manager was at when the person went out." While the expatriate is overseas, a member of the local senior management assumes responsibility as a "career manager or godfather role," to quote Austin. His duties include visiting the expatriate at work and discussing special concerns he may have about working in that country. Although the expatriate's performance abroad is assessed by the local supervisor, the reentry sponsor's comments generally prevail if there is a difference in opinion. In light of the board's emphasis on internationalizing the group's operations and the fact that expatriates are generally selected from the cadre of high achievers, however, most repatriates are promoted upon return.

Success and Reasons for Success

At ICI the rate of expatriate failure is around 6 percent. Some of these failures may be attributed to insensitivities to local cultures. For example, in Korea and Japan promotions are based primarily on seniority, not meritocracy. In these countries it may be difficult for local nationals to accept relatively young expatriates as their supervisors, however competent they may be.

Wooton indicated that the attitude toward living in a foreign environment often plays a pivotal role in determining the success or failure of an expatriate assignment. "If an expatriate goes abroad a little reluctantly because he has been told that it is in his career interest, or because he is needed, he may think he is doing the company a favor," Wootton explained. "His family did not particularly want to go, but is prepared to go with him. With that attitude, the family would like the overseas situation to be as similar to home as possible. They do not look for exciting differences. They try to find things that may resemble home as much as possible. But you won't find another country like home, so they are disappointed, get upset, and long to get home. In the case of a family that wants to go abroad, they look at all the strangeness as an opportunity to experiment and find out about other things. They will have a fantastic time there for a couple of years, will be able to overcome all the obstacles, and will come back with glowing stories about how wonderful it was." He cited the example of two expatriate families sent to ICI's Taiwan operation. The first family had no problem at all: "They loved the house, they thought the servant was wonderful, and everything was fine." When this family returned, a second was sent. To facilitate matters, the newcomer decided to use the same house, servant, and chauffeur. However, everything went wrong. Within weeks, the wife had dismissed the maid and was about to fire the chauffeur. The second family found every conceivable fault with the house. While the circumstances were identical in both instances, the attitude was totally different, and it ultimately accounted for the diametrically opposed outcomes in these two expatriate assignments.

If the expatriate is unable to perform his duties effectively in the foreign country, he may be recalled. In practice, however, the overseas subsidiary would "persevere with him as long as they possibly could, hopefully to the normal end of the tour of duty," said Wootton. Since the tour of duty at ICI is relatively short, lasting between two and three years, and the company allows for a "settling period where he would be given the benefit of a doubt and where it is hoped that things will change," by the time it becomes apparent that the individual cannot adapt to the local environment, there is not much of a term left. When the failure is attributable solely to family circumstances, it may not have an adverse impact upon the person's chances of future promotion within the corporation. In general, people at the lower levels of management can "slot right back in," whereas those who occupy senior levels of management and who are quite advanced in years may be given the option of early retirement.

When asked about the reasons for the relatively low rate of expatriate failure at ICI, the following explanations were proffered.

First, as noted earlier, most of ICI's overseas operations are well established. Consequently, expatriates are not moving into strange territories. This factor is enhanced by the second reason, namely, the existence of a strong corporate culture that serves as "the glue that holds the company together." Wootton said that an expatriate is "not going out among strangers, he is coming out to friends." Because of this strong corporate culture, managers from different countries can relate well and communicate with one another despite language and other nationalistic differences.

A third reason for success is that ICI allows a "settling period" in which due consideration is given to the fact that the expatriate is new to the foreign environment and work situation. This is similar to the practice in most Japanese MNCs (Tung 1984a). Fourth, the company carefully reviews the suitability of a candidate and his family for an overseas assignment. Quite often, people are eliminated from serious consideration if the family situation is deemed inappropriate.

Finally, in contrast to their American counterparts, most Britons have traveled abroad. About 60 percent of all Britons have taken holidays in other West European countries and elsewhere. Consequently, they have obtained greater exposure to foreign cultures and people. "Americans don't have the reputation of being outward-looking as compared to the Europeans," Rogers observed. Americans don't tend to go abroad on holidays as much as Europeans or even Australians. . . . All the facilities are pretty much standard throughout the United States—there are major shopping chains and McDonald's. In America, you can have everything that is different in climate and scenery, and yet all the things you are familiar with, and it is comfortable and comforting to be in that kind of situation. But once you get out of that situation into another country, then everything is different. For example, there is a concern about whether you drink the water."

At BP the incidence of expatriate failure is less than 5 percent. Austin attributed most of these failures to some form of family crisis or personality problem. He gave five reasons for the low rate of expatriate failure.

First, BP makes allowance for less-than-average performance in the first year of foreign assignment. In his words, the company is "fairly tolerant of the adaptation need." As noted in Chapter 1, exempting expatriates from demanding administrative duties in the first six months after arrival in the foreign country facilitates the acculturation process.

Second, the parentage system helps allay expatriates' concerns about possible problems of repatriation, thus enabling them to devote full attention to the overseas job. This factor is closely related to the third reason for success, BP's long history of operations abroad. The company has a large pool of experienced, in-house repatriates who can provide advice and assistance to newcomers about living and working in the host country.

Fourth, except for appointments at the senior management level, expatriate jobs are primarily in the exploration and production functions. These positions do not require extensive interaction with members of the local community.

Finally, the general ability of Britons to appreciate the "quasi-political niceties of doing business abroad," to quote Austin, contributes to their success. Americans tend to conduct business "at a much faster pace, with less understanding, patience, or tolerance of the social arrangements around the business that we [Britons] are used to," noted Austin. "Britons are great in talking socially at great lengths before getting to the hard sell or hard buy. . . . My view is that U.S. personnel have greater difficulty in adjusting to cultures because they have a more isolated view of the way business is done, and they are surprised and unable to adapt when they go to other countries." According to a manager at BPx International, Europeans have a wider perspective on the world. To highlight this distinction, he recounted the experience of "one of our best managers," who attended a six-week course at the University of Virginia (U.S.). This colleague was quite appalled to find so little attention devoted to international news events in the local newspaper. In a twenty-page newspaper, world news appeared only at the bottom corner of page 3.

The two managers at BPx International cited two additional reasons for the low rate of expatriate failure. First is the matrix organizational structure at BP, which requires strong interaction among BP centers worldwide. Consequently, the expatriate already has a good working relationship with the center to which he is assigned. Second is the economic situation in the United Kingdom. Because of the recession, which has been particularly hard on BP, the company has suffered substantial financial losses in the past five to six years. The U.K. staff has been reduced by 45 percent. "Under these circumstances, people are less ready to complain."

The impact of an expatriate's failure upon his subsequent career advancement at BP depends largely upon the reason for his poor performance abroad. According to Austin, if the person's performance returns to normal very quickly, the failure generally does not pose a problem. "But obviously, if somebody has a hiccup in his career, it requires closer examination in the future."

Proposed Changes

ICI currently guarantees reentry to the organizational level at which the expatriate left. Wootton would like to promise reentry into a higher position, so that there would be a greater incentive to serve abroad and a higher premium placed on an international experience.

Austin proposed a number of changes for BP's expatriation policies. He would like to place greater emphasis on language training "as an investment, rather than a direct link with potential overseas service." He would also seek to develop interpersonal skills at the more junior levels of management through a series of workshops on influencing skills and tactics, negotiation skills, and sensitivity training. At present, these courses are offered at the senior levels of management only. Austin also believes that the bureaucratic and administrative barriers to international transfers should be removed, specifically the high cost of expatriation, the quid quo pro system for international exchanges which may limit the international mobility of third-country nationals, and the problem of repatriation into the small associate companies.

4 ITALIAN MULTINATIONALS

This chapter examines the international human resource management programs at five Italian multinationals: three manufacturers and two banks. The three manufacturers are Fiat, the largest privately owned industrial group in Italy; Ing. C. Olivetti and C., S.p.A., a leading manufacturer of electronic equipments and products in the world; and Montedison, the largest chemical organization in Italy and the second largest private-sector company in the country. Together, these companies constitute the industrial backbone of the Italian economy. Of the banks, one is Instituto Bancario San Paolo, a financial institution that traces its origins to 1563 and that began international operations in the late 1970s; the other, which chose to disguise its identity, is a leading Italian financial institution that began its international operations more than a century ago.

Since the history of expatriation at Instituto Bancario San Paolo is very recent and the other Italian bank chose to disguise many vital statistics, this chapter will not present detailed write-ups of these two companies. Rather, the information on these banks will be incorporated, where relevant, throughout the chapter. The two interviewees at Instituto Bancario San Paolo were Ezio Cullino and Luigi Capuano, members of senior management in the bank's headquarters in Torino.

THE FIAT GROUP

The Fiat Group is made up of thirteen autonomous divisions or companies, including automobiles, commercial vehicles, agricultural tractors, construction, metallurgical products, civil aviation, telecommunications, engineering, railway equipment and transportation systems, tourism, bioengineering, thermal mechanics, publishing, and finance. In fact, the

Fiat Group is so pervasive in virtually all aspects of the Italian economy that it is often said, "Fiat is Italy." In 1983 the group's consolidated sales totaled 21,985 billion lire. That year was "one of the most testing years" in Fiat's operations since World War II because it marked the culmination of a three-year recession in the Italian economy, with declines of 1.5 percent and 8 percent, respectively, in the country's gross domestic product and industrial production over 1980 (*Fiat 1983*). In 1983 the group employed 243,808 people, down from 263,760 in 1982. While Fiat has over 200 production plants in nearly seventy countries worldwide, two-thirds of its operations are concentrated in Italy.

The information provided here was obtained from in-depth interviews with Vittorio Tesio, director of organization and personnel, and a member of his staff, Mr. Gianni. Tesio's department is responsible for formulating the compensation and expatriation policies and designing management development programs for the 3,249 managers within the Fiat Group. Fiat's overall policies are set by the central personnel function in the holding company in Torino but are administered by the respective companies. In most companies with overseas operations, there is a personnel abroad administration manager who is in charge of all expatriates. Tesio's office meets regularly with these managers, thus keeping his office apprised of all expatriation problems encountered by member companies.

Only 250 of the 3,249 Fiat Group managers are managed directly by the holding company. These 250 key managers are members of top management from each company in the group. About 50 percent of them occupy positions at the *direttori* (director) level. At Fiat, the level of *direttori* is over 1,056 Hay points. Their promotion, rotation, salary, and benefits are managed directly by the central personnel function of the holding company in Torino.

A distinguishing characteristic of the Italian industrial relations scene is the existence of the *contratto dirigenti*, a national contract governing all managerial personnel in the country. In Italy managers are referred to as *dirigenti* (over 600 Hay points). The base salaries and certain employee benefits of the *dirigenti* nationwide are established in a special contract negotiated once every two years between the managers' union and the entrepreneurs' association. There is a managers' union and an entrepreneurs' association for each major branch of economic activity in the country. The entrepreneurs' association to which Fiat belongs is the National Confederation of Industrial Companies. The compensation policy and benefits specific to a company are developed within the larger context of the *contratto dirigenti*.

Staffing Policies

As noted earlier, two-thirds of Fiat's operations are in Italy. Of the 243,808 employees, only 40,000 are employed outside of Italy and of these, 600 are expatriate staff (excluding those who go overseas for less than eighteen months). The geographic distribution of expatriate assignments is as follows: 174 in Europe, 166 in Latin America, and the balance in the rest of the world. Most of the top positions in Fiat's overseas operations are staffed by Italians. This is also true of both banks. At Instituto Bancario San Paolo, this practice may be attributed to the bank's being in the start-up phase of international operations, during which it is common to use parent-country nationals to establish a presence in the foreign market.

Fiat's policy is to select its top overseas managers from employees who have lived and worked in the foreign country for a long time. For example, the general manager of Brazil joined Fiat several years ago but has lived in Brazil for years. In fact, he was educated there and is married to a Brazilian national.

Expatriate assignments at Fiat fall into three general categories: technical, managerial, and career expatriates. Technical appointments generally involve employees below the managerial level and are made primarily for solving specific technical problems abroad, such as training of local personnel. These assignments do not exceed two years.

As do many multinationals, Fiat also makes assignments for career development purposes. The average duration of such assignments is from three to five years. According to Gianni, "the experience abroad is very important to the career of the employee." An estimated 15 percent of the expatriates who acquired international experience between 1974 and 1984 now occupy senior management positions in Italy. Tesio noted that the chairman of Fiat, Giovanni Agnelli, would like to develop a larger core of Italian managers with international experience, which can be acquired through expatriate assignments. This policy suffered a major setback, however, because of the economic downturn that affected corporate sales, thus delaying the repatriation of some employees.

Assignments at the senior management level extend for ten years or more. In fact, many people who assume such positions are career expatriates.

Since 1979, Fiat has reduced its expatriate staff from 900 to the present level of 600. Thus, 300 people had to be brought back to Italy. Due to the contraction of the Italian economy, however, Fiat was unable to deploy these repatriates in suitable positions upon their return. Consequently, some left to join other Italian companies that could utilize their international experience by placing them in the international circuit again. Any time an expatriation ends with a negative career move upon return, the problem tends to ripple, discouraging other individuals with high potential and aspirations from undertaking such assignments.

As Tesio pointed out, Fiat is not a multinational corporation in the fullest sense because 80 percent of its employees work in Italy and most of its operations are located at home. At one time, Iveco, the commercial vehicles division at Fiat, sought to internationalize its operations by designating English as the official language of the company and by bringing in foreign nationals. A matrix system was organized around the division's three primary operations in Italy, Germany, and France. The experiment did not succeed, however, because "Italians dominated the company," leading to problems of "cultural integration among the various organizations." The foreign transferees experienced difficulty in "integrating themselves into the Fiat model." The official language of Iveco has now been reverted to Italian.

Selection Criteria and Procedures

Fiat uses three major criteria in selecting people for overseas assignments: language proficiency, technical competence, and relevant previous experience. In assignments to Latin American countries, language is generally not a problem because Italians can learn Spanish and Portuguese very quickly. Consequently, for these assignments, the focus narrows to the criteria of technical competence and relevant prior experience. In one instance of selecting a senior manager for Brazil, these two criteria were key. Because the Brazilian operation was experiencing turbulence with the unions, the head office reviewed its personnel files to identify those with good track records in industrial relations and labor negotiations. From this list, the selection was narrowed to one candidate who also had solid financial skills and previous managerial experience in hyperinflationary economies like Brazil's.

Training Programs

Tesio indicated that Fiat provides only language training to prepare its expatriates for overseas assignments. For assignments to Latin America, expatriates undergo two months of language training in Spanish or Portuguese.

Other training programs provided at Fiat are not specific to expatriate assignments. However, since almost all expatriates take these courses as part of their overall career development, they are briefly described here.

Prior to 1984, group-wide training programs were reserved for only two categories of personnel: new recruits who have college degrees and employees recently promoted to the position of *dirigenti*. The new recruits enter a six-month program designed to familiarize them with Fiat's corporate history and the various activities they will be involved in as employees of Fiat. College graduates must work for a minimum of six to seven years before being promoted to the level of *dirigenti*. Upon appointment to the *dirigenti* level, they enroll in a one-month residential program at the company's training center located twenty-five kilometers outside of Torino. This program focuses on the general principles of management.

In 1984 Fiat initiated a program for the 250 top managers of the various group companies. This program is conducted in conjunction with the institutional meetings held annually in Torino to discuss the past year's activities and to review projects for the year ahead, and is attended by Giovanni Agnelli, chairman of the board, Cesare Romiti, managing director, and the managing directors of each company. The institutional meetings are followed by a six-day program held at Fiat's training center and run by in-house experts and professors from Harvard, Stanford, and Italian universities. Each year the program revolves around four different topics. In 1984 these topics were understanding the Italian and world economy; managerial skills and public speaking, including how to be interviewed and how to manage subordinates; understanding economic problems; and commercial problems in Europe. A participant can select any one of the four topics.

Group companies also send their senior people and employees with high potential to executive education programs such as INSEAD, the International Management Development Institute (IMEDE) in Lausanne, Switzerland and programs at Harvard and Columbia universities. In addition, the central personnel function, in conjunction with the management school, develops project courses for each company in the group. The management school, devoted to education and training, is a separate company within the Fiat Group.

Remuneration Policies

Upon expatriation, the Fiat employee comes under the local salary structure of the foreign subsidiary and is treated in the same manner as the local nationals. His Italian contract becomes dormant, although the company continues to pay his Italian pension fund. In addition, the expatriate receives various allowances, including housing, school, income tax differential, and foreign service allowances. The housing allowance is roughly equivalent to 10 percent of his local salary. If housing cost exceeds 10 percent of that salary, the company pays 75 percent of the excess amount. The foreign service allowance ranges from 20 to 40 percent of the person's home salary and is pegged to the degree of hardship encountered in the destination country. Fiat divides the globe into five categories on the basis of hardship. Category 1 includes most countries in West Europe. There is no hardship premium associated with assignments to this region. Category 2 includes countries such as Australia, Canada, and the United States. The distance from Italy is an important consideration here. The premium for assignments to countries in this category averages 4 percent. Category 3 includes most countries in South America, Hong Kong, Singapore, Poland, and the Soviet Union. The hardship premium here averages 8 percent. Category 4 includes countries such as Thailand, Pakistan, Algeria, and Colombia and has about a 12-percent premium. Category 5, encompassing postings to Angola, the Arab countries, Nigeria, Iraq, Zambia, and Zimbabwe, features an average 16-percent premium.

"Generally speaking, expatriates experience a much higher standard of living in the foreign country," Tesio reported. "When we send people abroad, they can afford a house or a villa which they may not have in Italy. They also have servants which they don't have here. They belong to exclusive clubs and can send their children to private colleges, which is almost impossible for them in Italy on an Italian salary. That's why people were very willing to go abroad, particularly in the early 1970s."

At Instituto Bancario San Paolo, it costs between $120,000 to $200,000 per annum to station an Italian family abroad. By comparison, U.S.

companies' average yearly cost for each expatriate family is from $150,000 to $250,000.

Repatriation

As noted above, the economic recession in Italy has necessitated a substantial reduction in Fiat's expatriate staff, creating problems of reabsorption into corporate headquarters. Tesio conceded that there are additional problems associated with repatriation, which is why the company maintains a core of career expatriates. According to him, "People who go on the international circuit generally become career expatriates. With few exceptions, they do not return to head office." Their motives for serving abroad revolve primarily around career and money. Although an expatriate may occupy a position abroad considered similar to the level of the domestic position he left, he usually assumes broader responsibilities in the foreign subsidiary. Thus, expatriation is a wise career move. Another motive for serving abroad is the attractive financial package discussed in the previous section.

Where expatriate assignments are undertaken primarily for career development purposes, repatriation is easier because the person has already been identified as a high achiever. After acquiring an international experience, he can be brought back to fill a position of greater responsibility at headquarters.

Success and Reasons for Success

According to Gianni, the rate of expatriate failure at Fiat is very low. He can recall only two or three cases in the past ten years. This number, however, is for the central personnel function, which is responsible for expatriating top managers only. "When we say the incidence of poor performance is low, this is for the holding company only," Tesio explained. "We have problems everywhere in managing people, but not with particular regard to the expatriate staff. . . . While Fiat has international problems in personnel, it is not a company with international activity in the sense that we have many people abroad. The problems are mainly in Italy. Most of our employees abroad are local nationals. So the problems that Fiat encounters overseas are generally local problems. This means that the problems are French problems, German problems, and Brazilian problems."

Gianni attributes the few instances of expatriate failure at Fiat to several reasons, including health factors, children's schooling, and family problems resulting from too much free time for the wives. Children's schooling poses a major problem. Few foreign regions have schools in which the language of instruction is Italian, meaning that the children of Italian expatriates would not be properly taught their native tongue, thus depriving them of part of their cultural heritage. Certain countries, such as Egypt and Iran, pose greater problems of cultural adjustment for Italian expatriates. However, Fiat's operations in these countries are limited in scale, employing very few people. Furthermore, in these areas, Italians establish their own enclaves to insulate themselves from the local environment.

Italian expatriates in Latin America, where Fiat has a significant presence, generally have no problem when living there, although they may experience hardship upon return. In Latin America the expatriate's ego is likely to become grossly inflated because of his status as an employee of a large Italian multinational. He becomes the subject of his employees' veneration and is treated like a celebrity wherever he goes. When he returns to Italy, he may experience difficulty in reassuming his former noncelebrity status. According to Tesio, "It takes about a year before their egos become deflated. But we don't have problems with people when they are there. Sometimes they don't want to come back unless we recall them."

Tesio and Gianni were asked to proffer some reasons for the relatively low rate of expatriate failure at Fiat, at least at the senior management level. First, they cited the flexibility of Italians. According to Tesio, "Generally speaking, we [Italians] are flexible. When Americans go abroad, they want to experience the American way of life in a foreign country. We enjoy Brazilian life or Argentinian life or American life." In other words, Italians appear to be more adventurous than their North American counterparts. This spirit of adventure facilitates adaptation in a foreign environmental setting. This theme echoes the point made by Wootton of Imperial Chemicals Inc. that attitude is a major determinant of success or failure in a foreign country. If an expatriate family seeks adventure and looks upon the foreign experience as a temporary phase in their life enabling them to learn about new ideas and places, they will be happy abroad and do well. In contrast, if they want the foreign country to be like home, they will be disappointed.

A second factor is the provision of a generous financial package for expatriates, enabling them to experience a higher standard of living abroad. This was discussed earlier.

Third, Fiat has a cadre of career expatriates for its international assignments. These people make a career of living in foreign lands and hence are adaptable to new environmental settings.

Finally, the overall qualification of Fiat employees is high. Since Fiat is the largest privately owned company in Italy, it is considered a very prestigious place to work. Consequently, the company can be selective in its recruitment. Of every 100 applicants for employment, Fiat accepts only the top 8 to 10.

THE OLIVETTI GROUP

Ing. C. Olivetti & C., S.p.A. is the world's leading manufacturer of electronic typewriters with 26 percent of total market share. It is also the major European producer of office automation and data processing equipments. In 1983 Olivetti's worldwide sales reached 3,736.2 billion lire, an 11.8 percent increase over 1982. Approximately 68.2 percent of these sales come from Europe (including Italy), 12 percent from Latin America, 8.1 percent from North America, and 11.7 percent from the rest of the world. Olivetti was selected as one of the ten best-run companies in the world in 1983.

Olivetti was founded in 1908 in Ivrea, Italy, by Camillo Olivetti. In 1929 it established its first overseas subsidiary in Barcelona, Spain. Today Olivetti has thirty-two foreign subsidiaries in an equal number of countries in Europe, the Americas, the Far East, and Africa. In 1983 it employed 47,800 people worldwide, 26,000 of whom were in Italy, 12,200 in the rest of Europe, 4,735 in Latin America, 932 in North America, and 3,906 in the Far East and Africa. About 6.6 percent of its overall workforce is engaged in research and development activities, 90 percent of which are located in Italy with the remaining 10 percent in California.

In 1983 Olivetti formed an alliance with the American Telephone and Telegraph Company (AT&T) in which the latter acquired 25 percent equity interest in the former. Through this linkage, Olivetti hopes to expand further into the fields of telecommunications and basic technologies, and AT&T gains access to Olivetti's data processing technologies and well-established international marketing network (*Olivetti 1983*).

The information provided here was obtained from interviews with four members of management at Olivetti's headquarters in Ivrea: Alberto Pichi, director for compensation procedures, Data Processing Group, and a twenty-five-year veteran of the company; Vincenzo Pedriali, education manager; Franco Mai, general manager, Latin American region; and Michael Rowley, a British national on assignment to the head office and assistant to the director, Far East and Africa region. Rowley is responsible for personnel matters in the Far East and Africa.

Staffing Policies

The expatriate staff at Olivetti is small. In 1983 there were 130 parent country nationals, 50 to 60 third country nationals, and 161 non-Italians on assignment to Italy. Since then these figures have remained fairly constant. While most Italian expatriates occupy managerial positions abroad, there is an increasing trend toward localization. In some countries, this practice may be difficult to implement because of a lack of local talent or because the local nationals may identify more closely with the host country than with corporate interest. Mai cited this as a specific problem in some of Olivetti's ten subsidiary operations in Latin America. "We feel that a local national tends to identify himself too closely with his country in terms of responsibility," he said. "Social relations may take precedence over business relations. Sometimes a managing director has to make unpopular actions, such as dismissing workers. This action is very difficult for a local national. It is not easy for an Italian manager either, but he identifies more with the company's interests rather than those of the host country."

Of Olivetti's thirty-two subsidiary operations, twenty are headed by Italians. The twelve headed by non-Italians are Argentina, Australia, Greece, Israel, Holland, Singapore, Hong Kong, Malaysia, Germany, Norway, Switzerland, and France. According to Rowley, in these subsidiaries the financial director generally is an Italian national.

While Olivetti seeks to evolve into a true multinational corporation, as yet there are no non-Italians on its main board, except for the AT&T people who were appointed to the board by virtue of the 1983 acquisition. To be promoted to the top positions in Ivrea, an employee must have years of experience within Olivetti since the company seldom recruits externally at the senior management level. Olivetti has recruited from the outside on several occasions but was dissatisfied with the results. Consequently, the company relies almost exclusively on internal promotions.

Olivetti's expatriate assignments fall into two general categories, technical and commercial. In technical assignments, expatriates generally assume positions as factory managers or R&D managers. The average duration of assignments in this category is three years or less. Approximately one-third of the expatriates are in this category. In commercial assignments, expatriates assume the top positions in the foreign subsidiaries for a minimum of four years in each country. Many commercial people are career expatriates. They "earn a lot of money and the lifestyle abroad is comfortable," explained Pichi. "Hence it is difficult to bring them back. In some instances, some individuals were originally sent abroad for two years, but if they succeeded in changing the subsidiary from a small- to a medium-sized operation, and then from a medium- to a large-sized operation, they may choose to live abroad for the rest of their lives. This occurs frequently among the commercial people."

Of the 161 transferees, that is, non-Italians on assignment to Italy, 110 stay in Ivrea for a very short time, either for training purposes or to serve as temporary assistants for jobs such as preparing documentation in non-Italian languages. The remaining 50 transferees stay in Italy for two to three years. At the time of the interview, Rowley was serving as a transferee in this category. When asked why he was appointed to the position, Rowley gave three reasons. One, he was formerly in charge of personnel at Olivetti (U.K.) for two and one-half years. Consequently, he has the background experience. Two, for career development purposes. As part of its internationalization effort, Olivetti seeks to appoint local nationals to senior management positions in its foreign operations. To qualify for these jobs, host-country nationals must be familiar with head-office operations and functions, and they can become so during the two- to three-year assignment in Ivrea. Three, Rowley believes that his British background gives him an edge in relating to people in the Far East and South Africa because of the colonial ties these countries once had with Britain. Presumably, it is easier for him "to understand the cultures in Hong Kong, Australia and South Africa as compared with an Italian."

Selection Criteria and Procedures

Olivetti uses several criteria to identify candidates for overseas assignments: the right person for the job, knowledge of the company's business, leadership abilities, adaptability, the family situation, language proficiency, and willingness to serve abroad. Each of these criteria is discussed briefly below.

Olivetti's policy is to find the right person for the job, regardless of age or nationality. As such, the company does not have a set policy of staffing the managing director positions in its overseas operations with Italians, host-country nationals, or third-country nationals. This is evident from the statistics presented earlier.

Knowledge of the company's business, including technical competence, is an important criterion. Since two-thirds of assignments fall into the commercial category, where an expatriate assumes a senior management position and stays abroad for extended periods of time, the candidate must be thoroughly familiar with corporate policy and practices. Such knowledge can be acquired only through long years of service with the company. When a subsidiary's managing director returns to Ivrea at budget time, he must answer questions posed by a corporate committee consisting of the managers of marketing, corporate planning, administration, and so on. He is cross-examined on all aspects of his company's operations, and he has to answer these questions without the assistance of any support staff. Consequently, he must be thoroughly knowledgeable about every aspect of the company's business. In assignments to Latin America, Mai indicated that the person must have a strong finance background to enable him to manage effectively in a hyperinflationary environment, where the local currency is subject to rapid depreciation and the cost of capital is high.

The candidate must also possess demonstrated leadership abilities. According to Pedriali, when the expatriate is assigned to a distant subsidiary operation, while the head office does not "lose control over him, he is certainly more independent. He must therefore be responsible, mature, technically competent, and know how to manage other people." Mai underscored the importance of strong leadership skills to successful performance in Latin America. He believes that in its South American operations, Olivetti needs people "who can be authoritative because, in South America, generally speaking, people follow the leader. They need to have a firm leader—maybe they don't love you, but they must respect you. This is fundamental. In South America, we need to have leaders who are like jumbo jet pilots with very long work experience and who are always under control, even in difficult and tragic situations." Furthermore, the person must have a strong psychological constitution. While Italians seldom have difficulty in adapting to the Latin American environment, some may fall victim to what he dubs as the "Latin American syndrome," a point also mentioned by Tesio of Fiat. The senior management expatriate is likely to be lavished with the adulation of his subordinates and near-celebrity status involving daily press coverage and socializing with the president and ministers of a country. "If the person is not psychologically ready," cautioned Mai, "he may be led to believe that he is more important than he really is. If a person loses his common sense and becomes psychologically imbalanced, quite often he makes mistakes in managing people. This is one possible danger in operating in South America. The person needs to have a strong psychological makeup. He has to be skeptical of false praises made by other people."

Adaptability to new environmental settings is a desirable quality in a candidate. Olivetti seeks evidence from his previous work experience that the person can relate effectively to foreign nationals. In Pedriali's words, "If somebody in Ivrea is in charge of personal computers for the Scandinavian countries, he becomes acquainted with the cultures of those countries. It is part of his work. It is quite natural for him to be assigned there because he already knows the market, the customers, the dealers, and so on." Pedriali outlined the typical career path of an expatriate as follows. The person is first assigned to a position that has dealings with a certain foreign subsidiary. For example, the person assumes the position of administrative auditor of the Spanish subsidiary. Through this association, he becomes familiar with the Spanish culture and legislative system. He travels to Spain several times and learns the language. After a while, he can be offered a position in a Spanish-speaking country in South America. He begins at a smaller subsidiary, say Venezuela, works there for a few years, and then moves on to Argentina. "It is a slow and progressive relationship with a given part of the world and with a specific culture. Through these various progressions, he can become managing director in the company for that region, and he may then return to a position in Italy."

Mai elaborated on this career progression, indicating it is difficult to prepare a person for a second-line management position by expatriating him to only one subsidiary. Generally, the person is rotated through various positions in several countries within the region. Postings can be across geographic regions as well. The present managing director of Olivetti's Japanese operation, for example, previously served in Venezuela.

A candidate's family situation must also be suitable for expatriation. In completing the annual evaluation form, an employee states whether he can undertake an overseas assignment and, if so, lists countries to which he would not relocate. The candidate also notes how his wife would react to a foreign assignment. (The wife will not be interviewed because such action is considered an invasion of one's privacy.) If the spouse has no reservations, then the employee will be expatriated. Pedriali said that in some cases, the wife remains behind either because she has a job or because of the children's education.

Children's schooling poses a problem because only a select number of countries in Europe and Latin America have Italian schools. In general, then, if a person has a very large family with children of varying ages, he will not be sent abroad. One Olivetti expatriate, after serving as administrative director of a foreign subsidiary for five years, requested to be repatriated, largely for reasons involving his children's education. Since there was no suitable position for him at home at that time, he was told to wait for a while. He resigned and returned to Italy, where he worked for another company for a year before rejoining Olivetti. "The main reason for his decision to return was that if his children had gone to university abroad, they would never have come back," Pedriali explained. "The man did not want to lose his family. He and his wife wanted to return to Italy to spend their old age and eventually die here. Had they remained abroad, their children would have become citizens of another country. So he requested the company to bring him back. The matter was so urgent from his standpoint that he resigned and joined another company." To address the problem of children's education, many career expatriates may consider the alternative of educating their children at American schools because when they move to a new location, they can always find another American school in the destination country.

The language proficiency criterion applies primarily to the European languages. The most popular foreign languages taught in Italian schools, in descending order, are English, French, Spanish, and German. While the person may not be thoroughly fluent in a foreign language upon graduation from high school, Olivetti invests heavily in language training programs. This is discussed in a subsequent section.

Finally, the candidate must be willing to serve abroad. As noted earlier, the person is always consulted about his willingness to live and work abroad. Declining an overseas assignment for a valid reason generally does not have a negative effect upon his candidacy for a senior position in the organization. It should be noted, however, that given Olivetti's emphasis on internationalization, international experience is considered an important requisite for advancement to senior management positions in Ivrea. Consequently, the person may limit his chances of promotion by not serving abroad. At present, approximately one-third of the top executives in corporate headquarters have served abroad for some years.

Training Programs

Like the Japanese multinationals, Olivetti invests heavily in the future of its employees by broadening their horizons through comprehensive training programs. It can afford to do so because the rate of turnover at the managerial level is low, between 3 and 5 percent. At the senior management level, there is virtually no job turnover.

Olivetti provides several types of training programs to develop an international orientation among its employees. These include the following.

Language Training.   As noted earlier, Italian students learn other European languages at school. In general, a person with this background would need four to six months of intensive training to become thoroughly proficient in the foreign language. Pedriali explained, "We do not send people to Britain for four to six months just to learn English, but if you put together all the courses that a person takes in four to five years, the individual is exposed to a total of four to six months of language training." Transferees to Italy are taught Italian. In the case of exotic languages such as Japanese, the individual can choose to learn the language if he so desires.

The International Executive Program.   Quoting Pedriali, Olivetti is "no longer international because we sell abroad. We are international because we want to be present in the global market with an internationally minded management. That is why our attention and efforts in the area of training are now geared toward the development of new programs designed to achieve this end." To that end, in 1984 Olivetti initiated two types of training programs, one at the top management level and the other at the senior management level. The course for top managers is known as the Olivetti International Executive Program and the one for senior managers is called the Olivetti Management Development Program.

The aim of the International Executive Program is "to strengthen and unify the critical mass of senior management who understand and are committed to developing and implementing the corporate strategy." In

1984 nineteen top executives in the Olivetti group attended the program. Of these, seven came from the foreign subsidiaries. The International Executive Program is a two-week program held at Olivetti's Haslemere Training Center, a residential facility for 150 people in Surrey, England. The program is organized around the following modules: managing corporate culture; competitive dynamics: global outlook and main actors; theory and practice of organization design; managing human and organization interfaces; technological innovation and business development; negotiation and conflict resolution; corporate communication process; cognitive and social aspects of decisionmaking; and leadership and group dynamics in high involvement settings. The case method approach is used.

Pichi was a participant in the 1984 program and recounted his experience as follows. "We lived together for a fortnight and we discussed a lot about the changes in the marketplace, pricing issues, et cetera. We spent seven to eight hours in class every day plus four hours in study groups. We were obliged to speak a common language, English." In his opinion, a major benefit of the program lay in the opportunity to interact intensively with people from other subsidiaries. As the director of personnel, he already knew most of the participants, but most of the other participants did not know one another. Consequently, "the seminar was very useful in integrating people from different subsidiaries and divisions."

In addition to attending the International Executive Program, Olivetti's most senior managers—namely, managers and executives who are close associates of the chairman of the board, plus senior commercial people who serve as managing directors of foreign subsidiaries—attend outside executive education programs, such as Harvard University's Advanced Management Program and programs at the Massachusetts Institute of Technology, Columbia University, and Stanford University. The average age of participants is forty to fifty, and they have worked with Olivetti for at least fifteen to twenty years.

The Olivetti Management Development Program.   This is a two-week program held at IMEDE in Lausanne, Switzerland, attended by thirty to forty first-line management personnel who work closely with the president of the company plus a select group of senior managers who work for the first-line executives. In 1984, Olivetti offered this program three times, at both IMEDE and Olivetti's Haslemere Training Center. It was conducted in English and attended by people from corporate headquarters and the foreign subsidiaries.

Both the International Executive Program and the Management Development Program are offered at regular intervals every year.

Olivetti does not provide in-house training programs at the middle management level. At this level, those with potential for further advancement within the company attend two- to four-week seminars in marketing, personnel, and manufacturing at business schools in Italy or elsewhere in Europe. The facilities used are ISTUD in Varese (near Milan), the Universita Bocconi (Milan), INSEAD (Fontainebleau, France), the London Business School (U.K.), and the International Management Institute (Geneva, Switzerland). Participants in these programs have worked with Olivetti for a minimum of ten years.

Olivetti offers a four-week in-house program for employees who have just been promoted to the level of *dirigenti*. Of the 26,000 employees in Italy, 600 are *dirigenti*, ranging between the ages of thirty and thirty-five. Olivetti recruits a senior faculty member from INSEAD to run this program.

Environmental Briefing. While Olivetti does not provide environmental briefings for its expatriates as a rule, there are exceptions. For example, the person who assumed the position of general manager of the Japan subsidiary attended a fairly long program at the East Asian Studies Department at Columbia University. At the time of the interview, Pedriali indicated that the company was considering providing some type of environmental briefing on a routine basis. In his words, "While I cannot say that we will do it, it is quite likely that we will sponsor something for different areas of the world. We are eager to learn what other companies do in this regard."

Remuneration Policies. As at Fiat, the Olivetti employee comes under the local salary structure upon expatriation. The home company continues to pay toward his pension fund in his base country. In addition, it pays an expatriate allowance to compensate for the cost-of-living differential and additional expenses involved in living and working abroad. Since most commercial people assume top management positions abroad, this move represents a significant promotion with a commensurate increase in salary, thus allowing them a very comfortable lifestyle abroad. Consequently, it is not necessary to offer a financial inducement to commercial expatriates. In fact, Rowley reported that "there is a demand for these senior jobs. . . . We don't put a financial inducement to go there. We put financial

inducements to perform—we give incentives to achieve certain results.''
This is tied in with Olivetti's management-by-objectives philosophy.

At Olivetti, a person is evaluated on his actual performance and his
potential. These are assessed separately. Approximately 20 to 50 percent
of the compensation plan is tied to actual performance. The income
differential between a person with high potential and one with average
potential is approximately 20 percent.

Repatriation

The director of personnel in Ivrea is responsible for managing the career
paths of top managers in the large subsidiaries, such as France, Germany,
Britain, Argentina, and Japan. Expatriates who occupy junior positions fall
under the jurisdiction of the personnel manager of the respective foreign
subsidiary. Those who have served very extended periods of time abroad
may encounter repatriation problems. For example, if ten senior managers
in the foreign subsidiaries all requested to be repatriated at the same time,
it would be difficult to find suitable positions for them in Ivrea. According
to Mai, "The internal structure in Italy generally cannot provide them the
same global responsibility they were used to before."

Generally, however, repatriation is not a major concern among
expatriates because of their positive attitude toward overseas assignments.
"In the case of a U.S. company, most Americans believe that the key
positions are at home. I think it depends on how you see your work," said
Pedriali. "I believe that going abroad helps to enrich oneself much more
than just remaining in Italy. It is useful in this company to stay abroad for
a number of years because Italy is not a big market like the United States.
So experiences in France, Germany, Britain, and the United States are
much more challenging—the expatriate learns more in the process. This
will become more important in the future. Our attitude toward working
abroad is more open." This theme was echoed by Cullino of Instituto
Bancario San Paolo: "For an Italian going to the United States, it is
considered as an enrichment of his professional career. . . . For me, going
to New York was an important move. For an [American] to move to Rome,
it is considered a serious problem."

At Olivetti there are two career paths for the commercial people: one
is within domestic operations and the other is abroad. "If you choose to
work abroad," explained Mai, "in most cases you have chosen a particular
way of life. Quite often, you accept the fact that you stay abroad for very

long periods of time, moving from one country to another.'' Expatriates are aware of the limitations associated with their career paths regarding movement back to corporate headquarters. ''They know,'' Mai said, ''that it is difficult for them to be reabsorbed into the mainstream of head office operations. . . . So when somebody is posted abroad, he severs his ties with his mother country, and the children have to follow along. I am obviously speaking in terms of Olivetti's practical examples. . . . We are very different from American companies. When you choose to go abroad, you have chosen to develop your career in a foreign country and generally you are not interested in returning to a career in head office. For example, in the case of the newly appointed general manager in Uruguay, he spent a few years as administrative manager in Venezuela and Mexico. It was a kind of training for his new position. He then moved as general manager to Uruguay, which is a very small subsidiary. What does this gentleman have in mind? He has no intention of returning to Italy to pursue a career in corporate headquarters. He plans maybe to move to Argentina, a more important position than Uruguay, and then from Argentina to Spain, again more important than Argentina, and then to France. If you consider that he stays four to five years in each company, he will have spent sixteen to twenty years abroad, at which point his career draws to a close. He has made this deliberate choice in life.''

One who goes abroad for career development purposes has no problem with repatriation if he is successful. According to Rowley, ''It is easy in a company that is expanding and is successful. We would not be so complacent if we were in a retrenchment situation. Where the company is expanding and growing, there is no problem in fitting successful people in.''

Success and Reasons for Success

Pichi recalled only two or three cases of expatriate failure in his twenty-five years with Olivetti. Similarly, Mai indicated that the incidence of expatriate failure in the Latin American region is very low. Pedriali attributed most failures to incompatibility in cultural systems and values, health reasons, and strains within the family.

The reasons for the low rate of expatriate failure at Olivetti appear to be many.

First is the international orientation of the Italians. There is a long history of Italian emigration to the United States and South America. In fact, approximately 40 percent of the population in Argentina is ethnic Italian. According to Pedriali, "While we are proud to be Italians because we wrote a part of the history of mankind and we contributed toward civilization, we are perfectly aware that other countries and cultures exist. We know that Italy is a small country. While we are born in this country, it is widely accepted that a person may have to leave." In general, Italians are curious to see foreign lands and meet members of other cultures. This is similar to the situation in Britain and Switzerland.

Careful selection of candidates also contributes to success. As noted earlier, Olivetti thoroughly reviews the person's qualifications and experience before expatriating him. As Pichi explained, "Generally speaking, we send abroad people who have international experience. If you have worked in a marketing department for six years, you have traveled all over the world for many years, hence you are adaptable to different ways of life. Perhaps your family has the inclination toward traveling and living abroad."

The provision of a comprehensive support network by corporate headquarters helps offset "the isolation of the expatriate," as Pichi puts it. Olivetti's expatriates maintain connections with the head office either through frequent trips home or through visits by people from headquarters. These visits occur at least four or five times a year and keep headquarters sensitive to the expatriate's needs and problems.

Olivetti's provision of comprehensive training programs prepares the expatriates for their new environments. While the company does not sponsor a regular program on cross-cultural encounters, Rowley reported that "our training programs involve the continuous development of a person in the jobs he has done before he is sent out to be a subsidiary managing director. We put a lot of time and effort into these people. We only promote successful people. If they have been successful to date, then they are considered for managing director positions abroad. So the failure rate is lower." In addition, with the increasing emphasis placed on internationalization, new programs have been implemented at the top and senior management levels to enhance this global orientation. These programs were described above.

The similarity in cultures in some destination countries also makes the adjustment period easier. As noted earlier, Olivetti has substantial operations in Latin America and, according to Mai, "Generally speaking, we are more similar to Latin Americans." An Italian can understand and be understood in Spain and other Spanish-speaking countries almost from the very beginning. Soon he can be thoroughly conversant in the language. "Hence there is a mutual understanding between peoples of these countries, with no problem in communication." In Latin America, it is common to encounter "irrational situations. . . . We are accustomed to irrational behavior, we can cope with irrational situations probably much better than Americans."

Tolerance of less-than-average performance in the first year of assignment allows expatriates time to become successful. As Harrari and Zeira (1978) found, the first six months is a critical period, and if the expatriate can be exempted from active duties, it will allow him adequate time to adjust to the foreign country.

The overall quality of Olivetti personnel also points to success. Of every 100 applicants for employment, Olivetti selects only the top five candidates. As a pioneer in providing social welfare programs for its employees, Olivetti attracts top people. Since the early 1940s, the company has provided housing for its workers, summer camps for children of employees, a company nursery for children under three years of age, and day-care facilities for children from three to five years old. While most of these social welfare functions are now provided by the Italian government, the company's traditional concern for its employees has translated into very smooth labor-management relations. Consequently, Olivetti was not subject to the labor unrest that plagued other Italian companies in the 1970s. According to Pichi, "Our style of management was very attractive to the young intelligentsia twenty-five years ago." In Italy, there is still a strong anti-industry sentiment. Since Olivetti was and is unique among Italian companies, "the intelligentsia were attracted to us. We are still able to maintain this good image." This is evidenced by the fact that in 1983 Olivetti was selected as one of the ten best-run companies in the world.

Finally, the willingness of corporate headquarters to accept ideas and suggestions from its subsidiaries makes for smooth interaction. Rowley cites flexibility as a distinguishing characteristic of Olivetti. In his opinion, as compared to Britons and Americans (he worked for a U.S. multinational prior to joining Olivetti), "Italians are extremely flexible. With American multinationals, you always feel it is the parent company that matters. . . . It is a different situation in Olivetti. We accept the fact that subsidiaries do things better in certain areas than we do in head office. We are quite happy to go to subsidiaries and learn that they are doing things which we are not and that they are doing them better." This attitude on the part of corporate headquarters enhances the attractiveness of an overseas assignment—an expatriate really has the opportunity to operate autonomously as long as he can show positive results.

THE MONTEDISON GROUP

The Montedison Group is the largest chemical organization in Italy. In 1983 its worldwide sales stood at $7.019 billion. That year marked an important turnaround in the group's net financial losses. In 1982 net loss amounted to 9.5 percent on sales; by the fourth quarter of 1983, this loss had declined to 1.1 percent. For several years, Montedison had incurred large financial losses attributable, in part, to the strong government intervention in the group's operations and affairs. After lengthy negotiations, an agreement was reached with ENI, the public chemical sector, under which Montedison would withdraw completely from the Italian public sector. Montedison transferred some of its plants to ENI and vice-versa. As a result of this consolidation, Montedison is now primarily in fine chemicals, while basic chemicals are controlled by ENI. This external consolidation was accompanied by an internal restructuring. Previously, Montedison had been one big company with many divisions. Now there is a central holding company with subholdings and operating companies below it.

The Montedison Group operates in three additional sectors: energy, services (including engineering, publishing, retailing, financing, and insurance), and basic chemicals (now largely under the control of ENI). Under basic chemicals, Montedison has joint ventures with Hercules, a U.S. concern, and other companies.

In 1983, 49 percent of group sales were derived from West Europe (including Italy), 9 percent from East Europe, 18 percent from Arab countries and Africa, 9 percent from North America, 2 percent from Latin America, and 10 percent from Asia and Australia. The group employed 73,000 people worldwide, 5,241 of whom worked outside of Italy in its sixty-five foreign subsidiaries.

The information presented here was obtained from in-depth interviews with Cesare Vaciago, director of key men and positions, as well as secretary of the management committee of the central holding company, and two members of his staff, A.S. Scarpallegia and A. Respighi.

Staffing Policies

Montedison derives a full 46 percent of its sales from outside of Italy. The group anticipates that most of its future growth will come from abroad, hence the current emphasis on internationalization. As part of its internationalization effort, Montedison's managers with international experience have been promoted to top positions at the senior management level.

Montedison has three levels of management. The highest level is referred to as "key people." Key people are considered as potential candidates for top management positions. There are approximately thirty to fifty such employees in the central holding company. Their average age is from forty-five to fifty. The second level is made up of three hundred managers who occupy senior positions at the subholdings and operating companies. According to Respighi, these people are considered as group resources "both in terms of mobility and career opportunities." The third level managers belong to the respective subholdings and operating companies. Those with high potential may be promoted within the group. Montedison has a policy of internal promotion and engages in external recruitment only as a last resort.

In 1983 Montedison had one hundred expatriates on assignments abroad. Most of these assignments were undertaken for career development purposes. Under the group's new policy, international experience is considered an important requisite for promotion to top management. Managers are encouraged to broaden their horizons through international assignments so they can eventually assume top positions in the operating companies and fill key positions in the central holding company. Some expatriates, such as those sent to the pharmaceutical division in the United States, are fairly young. Where expatriation is to foreign operations that are essentially trading units, the company generally sends more experienced people between the ages of thirty-five and forty.

The average duration of overseas assignment is four years, with certain exceptions. Assignments to Japan last a minimum of five years since it takes almost three years for the individual to become acclimated to the country's culture and environment; to recall the person earlier would be counterproductive. For assignments to hardship locations, the duration is shorter.

Given the group's current emphasis on internationalization, the Management Committee of the central holding company has formally guaranteed expatriates reentry. The level at which a person returns is entirely dependent upon his performance overseas. Success abroad almost always results in a promotion upon repatriation.

Where possible, foreign subsidiaries are managed by host-country nationals under the supervision of a non-resident Italian manager.

Selection Criteria and Procedures

Montedison uses several criteria for identifying candidates for overseas assignments, including language capability, technical competence, and spirit of internationalism.

Each candidate must be thoroughly conversant in two languages, English and Italian. English is required for all expatriates because it is the universal language of international commerce. Montedison also attaches great importance to knowledge of the host-country language. Respighi stated that expatriates must acquire proficiency in the local language if their assignment to that country extends for several years.

Since international assignments are considered an integral part of overall career development for those with high potential, it is only natural that they should be technically competent in their respective functions.

Having a spirit of internationalism means that the person and his family must adapt readily to new environmental settings. According to Respighi, "Italians are flexible—they don't insist on a particular type of food or housing. When our employees complain, they are actual problems and we solve them together." In assessing this spirit of internationalism, the suitability of the spouse is considered. As Respighi noted, "An international manager is a manager with an international wife because you cannot separate the couple."

Both Vaciago and Scarpaleggia maintain that, in general, Italian wives are adaptable and adjust readily to the local lifestyle. The wife's suitability for an overseas assignment is never gauged through formal interviews because such a procedure would constitute an invasion of privacy. Rather, the company avoids expatriating those employees with wives who work. This is consistent with the assertion made by Pedriali of Olivetti that Italian women who work are loath to leaving their jobs and would, therefore, most probably remain in Italy. Since prolonged separation of the couple could lead to family problems, Montedison avoids expatriating people with working wives.

When a vacancy for a foreign position occurs, a list of eligible candidates internal and external to the group is drawn up. Priority is given to those within the group because they are more knowledgeable about corporate policy and practices. The company recruits externally only if there are no suitable internal candidates.

At present, the group does not consult a person about his willingness to serve abroad. This is contrary to the practice followed at most multinationals, and Vaciago felt that the policy should be changed. Refusing overseas assignment has a negative impact on an employee's career advancement because international experience is a requisite for promotion to senior management positions. However, the company avoids harshly penalizing those who decline overseas postings for valid reasons, such as needing to care for aged parents.

Training Programs

Montedison utilizes both in-house and external facilities to prepare its people for overseas assignments. The following programs are used.

Language Training.   As noted earlier, for lengthy assignments, the company stresses knowledge of the local language. Thus it provides a comprehensive range of language training programs. The duration of a language program depends on the person's background knowledge. In some cases, refresher programs are adequate; in others, intensive training programs are necessary.

Area Studies Programs.   At the time of the interview, Vaciago indicated that Montedison is contemplating the use of the area studies programs offered by the Center for International Briefing, Farnham Castle (U.K.). When asked whether spouses will be included in such programs, he replied in the negative. "This will never be accepted in Italy. The wives here are very independent. Italian wives do not want to be contacted by the husband's company and be asked about mobility problems. No wife will accept to be trained. We don't interfere in the private lives of our employees."

To facilitate adaptation to a foreign environment, many expatriates leave their families behind in Italy for the first three months, during which they establish residence in the foreign country and make all necessary arrangements to facilitate the family's transfer abroad.

Remuneration Policies

Unlike at Fiat and Olivetti, where expatriates fall under the local salary structure upon expatriation, at Montedison expatriates continue to be paid their Italian salary. The company pays an allowance for cost-of-living differential. For assignments to difficult environments, a hardship premium is indexed to the cost-of-living in the country of foreign assignment.

Success and Reasons for Success

Vaciago reported that the incidence of expatriate failure at Montedison is very low. This can be attributed to several reasons.

First, the company has a fifty-year history of overseas operations and expatriation. Thus, like the British MNCs, most of its foreign operations are well established.

Second, according to Respighi and Scarpaleggia, Italians are flexible, adapting readily to local lifestyles and cultures. Respighi attributed this to the long history of emigration in Italy. "We are used to living abroad and working with people from different countries." This observation echoes that made by Pedriali of Olivetti.

Third, job movement in Italy is restricted. Vaciago noted, "We are a pleasant company to work for. In Italy, the chemical industry is not large. Hence there is very little competition. For an Italian chemical expert, the choice is between Montedison and ENI." Since Montedison is the largest chemical organization in Italy, it enjoys a virtual monopoly in the labor market.

Finally, the company makes allowance for less-than-average performance in the initial period abroad. This alleviates inordinate pressure for the expatriate to perform immediately on the job, which, as noted in Chapter 1, may hinder the acculturation process. In Tung (1984a) this allowance for a period of adjustment was also ascribed as an important reason for the low rate of expatriate failure among Japanese MNCs.

5 SWISS MULTINATIONALS

This chapter examines the international human resource management practices at five Swiss multinationals. While Switzerland is a small country, it is home to a relatively large number of multinational corporations with significant presence worldwide. It is informative to study how a small nation can make such successful inroads in the global economy. One of the five Swiss MNCs has chosen to disguise its identity and will be used here for comparative purposes only. The other four firms are the Swiss Bank Corporation, Sandoz Ltd., BBC Brown, Boveri, and La Roche.

THE SWISS BANK CORPORATION

Schweizerischer Bankverein (The Swiss Bank Corporation) is a leading Swiss bank with branch offices in the world's major financial centers, namely, London, New York, Atlanta, Chicago, San Francisco, Tokyo, Hong Kong, and Bahrain. It also has representative offices on five continents. In 1985 its assets exceeded $60.54 billion. The information presented here was obtained from in-depth interviews with Arnold Minder, vice president, and Guido Kurath, assistant vice president. Both men belong to the General Management—Staff Division, the unit responsible for overseeing the bank's expatriation policies.

Staffing Policies

The Swiss Bank Corporation employs 16,000 employees worldwide, 4,000 fewer people than the largest Swiss bank. Approximately 2,700 of these employees work in the bank's overseas operations. Its two largest foreign operations are London (established in 1898), with 1,000 employees, and New York (established in 1939), with 500 employees. In 1984 the bank had 300 expatriates, including 30 third-country nationals. This figure excludes Swiss nationals who are on two-year training assignments to the bank's major foreign operations. If these Swiss trainees were included, approximately 15 percent of the employees in the bank's foreign operations would be parent-country nationals. Unlike the practices at the British banks discussed in Chapter 3, in which the use of expatriate staff has decreased over the years, the number of expatriates at the Swiss Bank Corporation is expected to remain the same in the future to maintain the Swiss corporate culture. In Minder's words, "We will always remain a Swiss bank."

The Swiss Bank Corporation makes no significant distinctions in staffing policies between its operations in the advanced countries and in the less-developed nations. Rather, the differences in staffing policy are attributable to the functions and activities undertaken by the foreign operation. In the small operations, which are representative offices with ten people or fewer, the representatives are primarily Swiss. According to Minder, "The Swiss clientele expects to be received by a Swiss. This is general practice among many financial institutions." In the large units, such as the subsidiary operations in Panama, the Cayman Islands, the Bahamas, Australia, Monaco, Luxembourg, and Canada, and in the major branches engaged in the full spectrum of banking activities, such as London and New York, the nationalities of management personnel are mixed. For example, when the chief executive officer of the New York branch, an American, left the bank for family reasons in 1982, he was replaced by a Swiss national.

Similarly, third-country nationals are not employed only in a specific geographic region. Rather, they are distributed among the bank's foreign operations. For example, in its Bahrain operations, the bank has nationals from Germany, Luxembourg, and the United Kingdom. Similarly, there are Austrians in its Canadian units and Americans, Belgians, and Dutch in its London branch. The primary reason for using third-country nationals is that they are the best people for the jobs, all things considered. Swiss government restrictions on the issuance of work permits to non-Swiss nationals make it difficult to bring third-country nationals to the bank's head office in Basel for training purposes. Such training is considered essential in preparing third-country nationals for the responsibilities of senior management. To remedy this situation, the bank arranges quid pro quo exchanges of personnel when possible; in some cases it is necessary simply to limit the use of non-Swiss nationals.

The average duration of an overseas assignment is from three to five years. To avoid repatriation problems brought on by lengthy stints abroad, the bank prefers an expatriate to return home after completing two assignments abroad. There are exceptions, however. Some assignments to operations that offer standards of living comparable to Switzerland's may become permanent appointments. For example, there are twenty permanent expatriates in the United States and fifteen in the United Kingdom. Some expatriates choose to remain abroad because they can enjoy a higher standard of living and assume greater responsibilities as management personnel in a large foreign branch. The bank's preference, however, is for the expatriate to move to another country after five years and then return to Switzerland upon completion of the second assignment abroad.

To promote the development of an international perspective, the Swiss Bank Corporation uses cross-regional rotation of its expatriate personnel. The bank is organized into two geographic regions worldwide: one region consists of the United States, Europe, and Canada, and the second region consists of all other countries. Expatriates who have served in the Western hemisphere may be transferred to the Far East and vice-versa.

Selection Criteria and Procedures

The Swiss Bank Corporation uses several criteria to identify candidates for expatriate assignments. The first and foremost criterion is interest in serving abroad. The candidate is always consulted about his wife's willingness to live abroad. In some instances, his wife is included in the interview. Second is technical competence. Third is language capability. The primary languages required of expatriates are English, French, and German. Like most European multinationals, the bank does not expect its candidates to acquire facility in exotic languages such as Japanese. Fourth is adaptability to new environmental settings. The Swiss Bank has seven regional managers who travel to their respective regional offices two to three times every year. Consequently, they are knowledgeable about foreign conditions. Together with the General Management—Staff Division, these regional managers can accurately assess a candidate's suitability for assignment to a particular country.

If a person refuses an overseas assignment because of circumstances peculiar to a certain stage in his career, his future career advancement within the company is generally not negatively affected. However, given the importance of international experience, the person automatically eliminates himself for top management positions if he never serves abroad. Kurath noted that under the bank's management succession program, if a person aspires to the top ranks of management, he should have previous experience in a major financial center such as New York or London. Minder indicated that some people averse to serving abroad have resigned from the bank, recognizing that by serving only domestically, they may not be promoted as rapidly.

Training Programs

The Swiss Bank Corporation offers several types of training programs to prepare people for overseas work.

Technical Training.   There is generally a six-month to one-year lead time between the identification of a candidate and actual expatriation. Upon selection of the candidate, a technical training program is designed to remedy any deficiencies there may be in his skills and knowledge required for effective performance abroad. This program usually takes the form of on-the-job training that runs for six months to one year. For candidates to Latin American countries, this on-the-job training often includes a three- to six-month apprenticeship in the bank's New York office.

The bank also offers training in a broad range of subjects pertaining to international banking at its major branch offices in Basel and Zurich. An international banking seminar is held in the head office every January and February. Expatriates who do not have access to similar programs in their respective foreign locations may return to Switzerland to attend the program.

Minder hopes that in the future there will be a longer lead time between the identification of the candidate and actual expatriation to allow more time to brief candidates thoroughly about the demands and responsibilities of the foreign assignment.

Language Training.   Each expatriate attends a language training program, which averages from three to six months, depending on the person's previous knowledge of the language. In some cases, the candidate is sent to a country in which the language is spoken for intensive language training. For example, he may attend a three-month program in Britain to learn English. The bank encourages the spouse to learn the local language as well, to facilitate integration into the local community. The bank usually pays her tuition.

Cross-Cultural Training.   While the Swiss Bank does not provide cross-cultural training per se, it does emphasize the need for expatriates to learn about the foreign country and its people "systematically and thoroughly" before they go abroad. It encourages expatriates to read about the country and to engage in discussions with the regional managers and members of the Foreign Section, General Management—Staff Division. The Foreign Section is responsible for overall coordination and development of policies and programs pertaining to expatriation.

Management Training.   Since the Swiss Bank Corporation considers international experience an important requisite for promotion to senior management positions, expatriates may also undergo further training. Those with high potential for senior management attend programs at IMEDE (Lausanne, Switzerland), INSEAD (Fontainebleau, France), and other business schools. In addition, there is a program for future vice presidents of the bank consisting of a two-day lecture in January, a four-week component, and a one-week review session in September. This program is conducted by in-house managers and experts from the Banking Institute at the University of Zurich.

Remuneration Policies.

The Swiss Bank Corporation's remuneration policy applies to those transferred abroad for three or more years and enables them to enjoy a standard of living abroad comparable to that at home. For assignments to the United States and the United Kingdom, expatriates come under local contracts, and their salaries conform to those of local nationals hired for similar positions.

For assignments to other locations, the contracts are drawn up in the Basel office. Remuneration is calculated in the following manner. The annual income for a person holding a similar position in Switzerland is used as a basis, to which a regional allowance is then added. This regional allowance has two components: incentive and hardship. The latter is indexed to the living conditions specific to a foreign country, such as climate, political stability, cultural dissimilarity, infrastructure, language, isolation, and distance from the home country. For assignments to hardship locations, expatriates and their families are allowed annual rest and relaxation leaves in addition to their regular home leave. Moreover, the expatriate is reimbursed for differentials in income tax and housing costs between the foreign country and Switzerland. A company car is provided in most locations.

The regional allowance is limited to five years because the bank expects the expatriate to have adjusted fully to the local conditions after that time. If the person chooses to remain in the foreign country beyond that time, the regional allowance is terminated. There are exceptions, however. In the United States, for example, the rent subsidy may be continued since the bank does not expect the expatriate to buy a house.

Besides paying for travel, moving, and storage costs, the bank also grants relocation allowances, which are lump-sum payments made at the time of expatriation, upon transfer to another location, and again upon repatriation. These funds are intended to cover the purchase of special clothing, telephone installation costs, and other expenses associated with the move.

Success and Reasons for Success.

Minder indicated that the failure rate at the Swiss Bank Corporation is less than 1 percent. On average, there are only one or two instances of expatriate failure per year. These are attributable to health reasons or an inability to adjust to local environmental conditions. Countries that pose the most adjustment problems for Swiss nationals are those located in the Middle East and the Caribbean because of the isolation factor and the hot climates in these regions.

Minder and Kurath gave three reasons for the low rate of expatriate failure among Swiss Bank's employees.

First, they cited the importance of acquiring international experience. As noted earlier, overseas experience in a major financial center abroad is a requisite for promotion to the top ranks of the company. Thus, employees are eager to make a success of their foreign assignments. According to Kurath, "Normally for young people who serve in New York, London, and Canada, it is understood that they will be promoted soon after their return home." This echoes the point made in Chapter 3 by Hurst of National Westminster Bank.

Second, the bank exercises great care in selecting people who are suitable for overseas work. Candidates must have several years' experience, an average of five years minimum, with the company before being assigned abroad. Hence the bank has ample time to assess their strengths and limitations. In addition, given the premium placed on international experience, many of its employees are willing to serve abroad. Therefore the company can afford to be selective.

Finally, expatriates are given six months to adjust to the local environment. This policy facilitates adaptation.

THE SANDOZ GROUP

The Sandoz Group is a leading Swiss manufacturer of chemicals that derives 95 percent of its sales from abroad. In 1911 Sandoz established its first foreign subsidiary in the United Kingdom. Now it has subsidiaries in twelve countries and joint venture operations in many more. The single most important market for Sandoz products is the United States. In 1983 the group's consolidated worldwide sales reached 6,546 million Swiss francs. Approximately 43 percent of its sales came from Europe, 30 percent from the United States and Canada, 15 percent from Asia, 8 percent from Latin America, and 4 percent from Africa and Australia. The company is organized around five major product groups: pharmaceuticals, food, seeds, agrochemicals, and dyes.

The information presented here was obtained from in-depth interviews with Louis Eberle, group personnel manager, and Hans Kilchenmann, head of management development at corporate headquarters in Basel, Switzerland.

Staffing Policies

In 1983 Sandoz employed 38,109 people worldwide, 7,000 of whom were domiciled in Switzerland. The group has approximately 350 expatriates including third-country nationals. A breakdown of the nationalities of its expatriate staff is as follows: Swiss (70 percent), Germans (9 percent), French (9 percent), Britons (7 percent), and others (5 percent). The reasons for using third-country nationals are primarily twofold: one, for career development purposes and two, because of work permit restrictions. It is still easier to send a Briton, as compared to expatriates of other nationalities, to Canada because of Canada's commonwealth status. Third-country nationals are also used extensively in the Middle East.

Sandoz began its policy of expatriation, on a limited scale, before World War II. The number of expatriates increased dramatically in the 1950s and 1960s and, unlike at most multinational corporations, the use of expatriate staff has not decreased over the years. According to Eberle, this is because Sandoz "did not have a large number of expatriate staff to begin with." At present, only 27 percent of management positions abroad are occupied by Swiss nationals. Of the twenty top management positions abroad, 10 percent are staffed by host-country nationals.

In operations that use many expatriates, there have been attempts to reduce their number, both to save costs and to comply with the localization policies of the host governments. In Brazil, for example, the number of expatriates has dropped from a one-time high of more than thirty to its present level of twenty-five.

The majority of expatriates occupy positions as members of top and middle management. Some engage in specialist functions. A small minority serve as trainees. The duration of these latter postings is between two and three years.

Eberle said that there is no specific policy governing the duration of overseas assignments. Some expatriates who went out in the 1960s have remained in their foreign posts ever since. In the past fifteen years, however, the typical term of an overseas assignment has been five years. In assignments to hardship countries, such as Nigeria, the stay is three years or less.

In the past, the Swiss Bank Corporation has had some problems with repatriation. For this reason, Eberle urges expatriates to maintain close contacts with their superiors in corporate headquarters. "I tell them that they must discuss their wishes and preferences with their superiors back home. There is no point sitting and waiting in a foreign country until somebody in Basel thinks of them, because that will not happen. They must remind headquarters. People who did that met with a certain amount of success and they almost always got decent jobs when they came back."

Repatriation problems for candidates for top management positions have been largely eliminated through the centralization of the management development function in 1983. This function oversees the career paths of some 200 people slated for the 140 key positions in the company. The average age of these people is forty-two, and they come from various divisions throughout the world. While the members of the Executive

Committee are primarily Swiss, for the past fifteen years, foreign nationals, including a French and an Italian national, have also been on the committee.

Because most of Sandoz' business is derived from abroad, international experience is considered an important requisite for promotion to top management. Therefore, virtually all of the 200 people qualified for the 140 key positions serve abroad at some stage. In fact, when recruiting young managers, the company specifically asks whether they are willing to serve abroad. If they are not, they will not be hired.

Selection Criteria and Procedures

Sandoz uses several criteria to identify the appropriate candidates for overseas assignments: technical competence, communications skills, language proficiency, relational abilities, past performance, willingness to work abroad, flexibility, a suitable family situation, and health. Since the candidates have at least two to three years experience with the company, they can be assessed on these attributes. Furthermore, many of the candidates have served on special projects abroad for several weeks, so the company can gauge their ability to interact with members of foreign cultures. According to Eberle, "Past performance is very important. If a man is successful in dealing with peoples of other nationalities, then we think he is suitable."

In addition, the company uses Geert Hofstede's (1984) conceptualization of culture along four different dimensions (masculinity-femininity, individualism, uncertainty avoidance, and power distance) to assess the candidate's suitability for a specific country. Regarding language capability, like most European MNCs, Sandoz seeks candidates with proficiency in the European languages, such as English, French, German, and perhaps Spanish.

In the past, acknowledged Eberle, Sandoz seldom considered the constraints on a candidate's mobility imposed by his children's education. Since most Swiss are averse to sending their children to boarding schools, many candidates preferred to remain at home. This problem has been largely rectified by increasing the company's awareness of its employees' home situations. The annual assessment forms now request and specifically ask the employee whether he is currently ready to go abroad.

For assignments to tropical countries, the candidate and his family undergo a medical examination at the Tropical Institute in Basel to determine their suitability for living in hot and humid climates.

The candidates are selected by the division heads in Basel. In the Pharmaceutical Division, for example, there is a center that assesses twenty people annually to identify appropriate candidates from among them.

Training Programs

After being selected for an overseas assignment, the candidate and his family are sent to the destination country for ten to fourteen days to become familiar with its housing and schooling situations. Upon their return the company arranges for previous expatriates to the destination country to brief them on living and working in a foreign land.

Cross-Cultural Training.   If time permits, the company sends the candidate to the cross-cultural training programs at Farnham Castle (U.K.) or the Carl-Duisberg Center (Bad Boll, Germany). Although time constraints permit only a small minority of the expatriates to attend these cross-cultural programs, those who have gone considered the training very useful. Eberle hopes that in the future there will be a longer lead time between the announcement of a foreign position and the actual expatriation so more candidates will have time to attend these programs. The present lead time is only three to six months. Candidates who cannot attend these cross-cultural programs are given informational material prepared by the Employee Conditions Abroad Limited (U.K) and Bundesverwaltungsamt, a similar agency in Germany.

Language Training.   In assignments to countries with exotic languages, Sandoz may send the person to crash courses in the language. There is some concern, however, that knowledge of such a language may limit the expatriate's subsequent mobility, thus restricting his development as a manager. Kilchenmann cautioned, "It is good if an expatriate knows Turkish, for example, but we should be able to use him in other parts of the world as well." Spouses are generally included in the cross-cultural training and language programs.

Management Training.   Since international assignments are an integral part of overall career development for those who show high potential for senior management positions, the other types of management training programs at Sandoz will also be discussed briefly.

Almost all new employees who are university graduates, including those with MBAs, join Sandoz at the lower management level. The objective at this level is to develop management and leadership skills primarily through on-the-job training. This training is supplemented by a fifteen-day classroom-type program conducted over a three-month period. Since the mangement development function is decentralized below the level of candidates for top management positions, most countries offer their own training programs. If in-house facilities are not available, employees are sent to local business schools. The management development function at Basel custom-designs programs for the company's various divisions at all levels of management. In 1984 it offered thirty different programs to suit the specific needs of the various divisions.

In-house programs are supplemented by outside courses. Sandoz employees engaged in research and development maintain close contact with universities and attend special R&D courses at the International Management Institute (Geneva, Switzerland), the Management Center Europe (Brussels, Belgium), and the Massachusetts Institute of Technology (Cambridge Mass, U.S.A.). People at the upper management level attend the four-week program at INSEAD (Fontainebleau, France) or the eleven-week Advanced Management Program at Harvard University (U.S.A.). At the top management level (i.e., members of the Executive Committee), people attend one-day seminars on special topics, such as information technology, sponsored by the Management Center Europe.

In the past, employees were sent to management development programs before they were given specific assignments. As a result, when some people were not given appointments that utilized their newly acquired skills, they were disappointed. The company has now rectified the situation by sending people to outside courses immediately prior to a new appointment.

Remuneration Policies

Like those of most MNCs, Sandoz' compensation package for expatriates includes a cost-of-living differential, an income-tax differential, and housing and school allowances. In addition, there is an expatriation allowance that includes foreign service and hardship premiums. The expatriation allowance ranges from 25 to 70 percent of the net base salary. Unlike the Swiss Bank Corporation, where the foreign service premium is discontinued after five years, the expatriation allowance at Sandoz is given as long as the person remains overseas. The rationale for paying this premium indefinitely stems from the fact that the person remains in a foreign country by virtue of his doing a good job there. "Consequently," Eberle explained, "it may demotivate him if we take away a part of his salary, even if it is called a foreign service premium." However, in cases where the company wants to repatriate a person but that individual prefers to stay in the foreign country, he is given the option of remaining there on local terms, except for a continuation of his Swiss pension scheme, or returning to Switzerland.

Success and Reasons for Success

At Sandoz there have been only three cases of expatriate failure in the past twenty years. These failures can be attributed to the inability to adapt to the local culture, on the part of either the expatriate or his family.

Eberle and Kilchenmann gave several reasons for Sandoz' low rate of expatriate failure. These are discussed below.

First, Eberle observed that "the Swiss are particularly adept for international careers because we have been international all the time. Our ancestors went to war abroad. This is in our blood. I think this is one reason why we have few failures. It is not because we do a better job in preparing them—we do very little to prepare them for a job in a particular country. I myself worked at one time in an exotic country and I wasn't prepared at all, but you just try to adapt without being told."

This ability to adapt to new environmental settings was elaborated upon by an executive of another large Swiss MNC interviewed for this study.

> The Swiss make the assumption that if a person has a determination and will to survive, that is the way they get along. It is part of the Swiss tradition that they don't pay attention to these things. To move from the German part of Switzerland to the French part of Switzerland, you have to go into a completely different school system with a completely different language. So it takes you about three years to adjust over there. We don't do anything in the French part of Switzerland to integrate the Germans. You just go over there. By extension, you don't do anything for the French, the Britons, or anybody else. . . . I really think it has an awful lot to do with their personal

attitude on life. If you moved here, you might spend three years before you know your neighbor. By heritage, the Swiss are able to survive in quite an isolated place. This means that you can send them to Paraguay and they can just be as happy as they are here.

This executive attributed the survial instinct to the history of emigration.

There was a period before and after the war where it was common for people to pack their bags and go somewhere else. In some of the farm communities, they have the system of ultimogeniture where the youngest in the family inherits the land, so all the older ones have to emigrate. Except for the chemical and watch industries, there really wasn't much going on around here. So for years, they were either running hotels or trading or going somewhere. They go out and like it there. They are very tough. In Switzerland, nobody invites you to dinner. It is expected. The Swiss are emotionally equipped to live abroad, they are self-sufficient, and they are practical. Physically and emotionally, they are quite resilient. Since they have the tradition of goint out, making their fortune, coming back, and buying a house, they don't raise hell about what they have got in a foreign country.

Second, since most Swiss are multilingual, language generally does not pose a major problem. As a nation, Switzerland is very diversified, a conglomeration of German-, French-, and Italian-speaking people. According to the executive of another Swiss multinational, "The Swiss expect all normal people to speak four or five languages." The assumption is that if a foreign language is required, the person can learn it with little difficulty.

Third, because of the aforementioned two reasons, the Swiss are generally not ethnocentric in their orientation toward people of other cultures. Kilchenmann pointed out that the Swiss do not establish enclaves abroad, nor do they seek to impose their value systems and perspectives on people of other countries.

Fourth, in general, the Swiss are quite loyal to their companies. Compared to their U.S. counterparts, the rate of job turnover at Swiss companies is low. When the level of commitment among employees to organizational goals is high, they are generally more tolerant of unpleasant circumstances that may arise in the course of an overseas assignment. They are dedicated to making the foreign assignment a success.

Finally, Sandoz allows the expatriate six months or more to adjust to the local situation. The company is cognizant of the ill-will the local community might harbor toward the company if the expatriate were unable to adapt to the local conditions.

Another reason for the low rate of expatriate failure at Sandoz and other Swiss multinationals, not specifically identified by Eberle and Kilchenmann, is the importance these companies place on their overseas operations. As noted earlier, approximately 95 percent of Sandoz' sales are derived from abroad. In the words of an executive of another large Swiss MNC, "Out there is where the business is. It doesn't mean that the jobs back home are unimportant, but it puts a somewhat different tenor on where the important jobs are." This is very different from the situation at most U.S. multinationals, where the plum positions are in corporate headquarters. Hence people who aspire to higher positions within the company often desire to serve extended periods overseas. In companies like Sandoz, where the majority of sales and profits come from abroad, there may be a "lot of Swiss out there who would never dream of coming back" because of the broader responsibility, large earnings, and prestige associated with overseas postings.

BBC BROWN, BOVERI & CO., LTD.

BBC Brown, Boveri & Co., Ltd. (or BBC for short) is a leading international supplier of electrical equipments and provides a wide range of industrial services worldwide, including engineering, turnkey projects, financing, and local manufacturing. The BBC Konzern is made up of three regionally structured parent groups—Swiss, German, and French—and their companies. The Swiss group was founded in Baden, in 1891; the German group was established in Mannheim, in 1900; and the French group was established in 1901. The top executive body is the Konzern Managing Committee, which is composed of the chairman of BBC, the chief executives of the three major national companies, and the heads of two groups of smaller BBC companies. The latter include a medium-sized manufacturing company and a sales and assembly subsidiary. Each member of the Konzern Managing Committee is assigned a line function (i.e., management of a group) and/or a strategic function, such as marketing, finance, planning, and technical strategy.

The Konzern is headquartered in Baden. In 1983 its sales reached 10,700 million Swiss francs, a 10 percent increase over the previous year, and it employed 90,600 employees worldwide, down from 94,100 in 1982. The geographic distribution of its employees is 78,380 in Europe, 3,600 in North America, 4,970 in Latin America, 1,240 in Africa, 1,330 in Asia, and 1,080 in Australia. Exports account for 38 percent of consolidated orders received by the Konzern. ("Consolidated orders" are purchases of engineering services and manufactured products from the various members of the Konzern.)

During World War I, each national company was forced to operate separately to survive. The independence of the national companies was reinforced after the war by the protectionist barriers, economic problems, and political instability in many European countries. Today, the national companies are autonomous in their operations but are subject to broad policy guidelines set by the Managing Committee of the Konzern.

This case study focuses on the international human resource management practices in the Swiss group. Throughout the years, the Swiss group has maintained a clear technological lead among the various national companies. The group employs 19,900 people worldwide. Between 72 and 86 percent of the group's orders are for the export market. The information provided here was obtained from an in-depth interview with Hans Beat Gamper, an executive in charge of human resource management policies in the Swiss group.

Staffing Policies

BBC began its policy of expatriation (i.e., sending people to countries outside of Switzerland, Germany, and France) between the two world wars. In 1983 the Swiss group employed 450 expatriates, 50 of whom were third-country nationals. Many of the third-country nationals come from Germany, the United Kingdom, and Holland. Third-country nationals are used when they are the best people for the positions and for management development purposes.

The majority of expatriates occupy positions at the top two levels of management in the group's overseas operations. In operations that cannot be adequately staffed using local nationals, some expatriates may be engaged for assembly functions. The number of expatriates has remained fairly constant over the past five years for two countervailing reasons. On the one hand, because of the expansion of its overseas business and activities, the company has had to establish more subsidiaries abroad. In the start-up phase of an operation, it is deemed imperative to use parent-country nationals. On the other hand, expatriates are being replaced by host-country nationals in countries where the local educational standards have risen. Many Swiss expatriates were sent to Brazil, for example, when the subsidiary was started up. With the subsequent establishment of good universities there, many expatriates have been replaced by Brazilian nationals. Gamper noted that this situation also holds true for some parts of Africa. In Nigeria, for example, local nationals have been promoted to management positions since the late 1970s.

BBC's policy is to use host-country nationals where possible. "Our company is unique," observed Gamper. "We are extremely decentralized. While it is fashionable to say that a company is decentralized, we are truly so from the very beginning—we have been decentralized for some fifty years now. Since very few directives are issued from corporate headquarters, we prefer to have people who know the local market." Since most of its customers are nationalized enterprises, such as power plants and public utilities, it is preferable to use local nationals to interact with their public-sector customers. The majority of BBC's operations in the industrialized countries and Latin America are headed by local nationals. In Brazil, for example, the entire management team, except for the finance manager, is made up of host-country nationals.

At BBC the expatriate function is decentralized for levels below that of chief executive officer. For assignments at the middle management level and below, headquarters merely serves a brokerage function in matching companies that can supply expatriate personnel with those units that require their services. At these levels, the final decisions are made by the respective companies.

The average duration of expatriate assignments in the management category is six years. Until recently, BBC did not guarantee that it would repatriate a person upon completion of an overseas posting. In 1982, however, the Konzern Managing Committee established a policy governing international transfers, binding on all companies of the BBC Konzern, that stipulates the organization which initiated the transfer must provide a written guarantee to repatriate the person at his previous level, at the very minimum, upon his successful completion of overseas services.

Gamper indicated that most Swiss are willing to undertake extended periods of overseas assignments for three reasons. One, since Switzerland is a small country, many Swiss seek employment with companies that can offer them an opportunity to see the world. This echoes the sentiment expressed by executives of other Swiss multinationals as well. Two, the overseas salary is good. Receiving an overseas allowance and a hardship premium in difficult locations also helps an expatriate family to put some of its money into savings. Three, a written corporate policy stipulates that in order to qualify for promotion to BBC management positions, the person must have "spent some time in a Group company abroad." The document goes on to state that "out of two similarly qualified candidates, preference should be given to those who upon their return will have the chance to use the international experience acquired . . . rendering them fit for promotion" ("Management Development in the Brown Boveri Group" 1977).

Foreign nationals are transferred to Switzerland and other group companies for training and to become familiar with corporate philosophy and functionings. Every year there are approximately thirty international transferees, the majority of whom come from developing countries. Their average age is thirty-two, and the duration of their assignments is typically three years. For very specific training, such as learning about electronic equipment for the shipbuilding industry, the duration is shorter.

Selection Criteria and Procedures

At the time of the interview, the company had just developed a weighted profile of the attributes required of candidates for managerial positions in a BBC company. These attributes include knowledge of corporate policy, functional skills, personnel administration skills, negotiating skills, and knowledge of foreign languages. Additional intellectual requirements include mental agility and the ability to separate the wheat from the chaff. In terms of character requirements, the candidate must exude confidence and maturity, show willingness to accept responsibility, and be adaptable to new environmental settings. He also must be "enthusiastic about the host country and its people" and have experience abroad.

To assess adaptability, the company does not administer tests but asks the employee about his willingness to live and work abroad. The wife's opinion is also solicited. In addition, the ages of the family's children are taken into consideration. As executives of other Swiss MNCs noted, Gamper indicated that Swiss expatriates generally have no problem in adapting to foreign countries. However, because of the problem of children's education, most Swiss are not mobile at certain stages in their careers. People with high school-aged children are particularly difficult to expatriate unless there are German and Swiss schools in the destination country. If such schools are not available, it is virtually impossible to expatriate these employees. "For Britons, it is perfectly normal to send their children to boarding schools. In the case of the Germans, it is easier. For the Swiss, the families keep the children until they finish high school."

While BBC places a heavy emphasis on international experience, it has adopted a flexible policy toward those who, for valid reasons, are not able to undertake an overseas assignment. In fact, two of the six members of the Konzern Managing Committee have never served abroad. They have, however, held positions that gave them experience in dealing with national and international problems.

When an overseas position becomes available, the company recruits either internally or externally. For internal recruitments, there are essentially two methods: (1) the Konzern writes to all companies and divisions to solicit their nominations of candidates or (2) an employee interested in the overseas position contacts headquarters directly or requests his supervisor to nominate him for the job. Candidates must have several years of experience with the company.

External recruitment is done infrequently. For sales and technical positions, the company needs people who are familiar with its product lines and services. Thus external recruits are hired primarily for staffing finance and bookkeeping positions.

Training Programs

BBC provides several types of training programs to prepare candidates for overseas assignments.

Language Training.   The company uses both in-house and external facilities for language training. According to Gamper, most Swiss like to learn foreign languages, so there is generally no problem in this regard.

Cross-cultural Training.   In 1983 BBC designed an experimental two-day seminar on cross-cultural encounters. This was an in-house program organized by an outside consultant in Zurich. While the experimental program was quite informative most participants felt that it was too short. Therefore, the company plans to extend the program to four days and to include spouses in the training. The small number of people requiring such programs at BBC makes it impractical to schedule them on a regular basis. Consequently, Gamper is considering the use of external facilities such as the Center for International Briefing, Farnham Castle.

Technical Training.   Professional training is provided, where necessary, to compensate for a candidate's deficiencies in technical knowledge and skills required for the job abroad. Courses and on-the-job training are offered.

Management Training. Since international experience is an integral part of overall development for BBC's higher management personnel, the general management training programs will also be reviewed briefly. "Higher management personnel" refers to "all members and potential members of the upper hierarchical grades in a company or group" ("Management Development in the Brown Boveri Group" 1977).

Broadly speaking, training is provided for two primary purposes: (1) to improve the job performance of existing managers and (2) to develop promising candidates for higher management positions. The company formulates certain objectives, assesses a candidate's potential in terms of these objectives, and then designs training programs to help him attain these goals.

The Konzern offers two central courses. One is a six-week program for sales engineers, both domestic and international. This course is taught in English at Baden and includes field visits to operations in Germany, France, and Italy. The other is an international management seminar attended by the top four hundred management personnel in the Konzern. Participants in this seminar include the heads of small companies, second-level management personnel in medium-sized companies, and third- and fourth-level management personnel in large companies. The international management seminar is a twelve-day program designed to promote international cooperation in individual fields of responsibility; discuss corporate policy and management principles and their application; discuss economic, social, and political developments worldwide and assess their implications for future policy changes; and promote a common doctrine and develop an international esprit de corps among members of upper management in the Konzern. The seminar is run by in-house specialists and professors from IMEDE and IMI. To facilitate greater interaction among participants and members of the Konzern Managing Committee, at least two members from the latter group serve as cochairmen of the sessions. At the time of the interview, an international BBC management symposium was being planned as a follow-up to the international management seminar.

Corporate headquarters also encourages subsidiary companies to sponsor their own training programs designed to meet their specific needs. In countries such as Switzerland, Germany, Norway, Italy, and Austria, training is an important part of the management development programs, which are offered independently of headquarters. The larger companies generally sponsor in-house programs. The Swiss group, for example, offers in-house programs at all levels. In addition, it uses outside agencies.

Every year, the Swiss group sends five people to the Swiss School of Management in Brunnen for a nondegree program that examines the special problems and issues facing Swiss managers. The Swiss School of Management is not an international institute like IMEDE or IMI, but an exclusively Swiss institution. BBC's Swiss group also encourages its people to interact with the local universities. For example, the group's scientific and management personnel lecture at universities, and the company donates scientific equipment to local engineering schools. Gamper observed that this close relationship between the academic and business communities is similar to that in the United States but dissimilar to the situations in France and Germany.

The smaller BBC companies generally lack adequate resources to offer in-house programs, so they rely primarily on external facilities. At the time of the interview, Gamper indicated that the Konzern was contemplating the introduction of central courses for middle management personnel. If implemented, they would be a resource to the companies located in countries that do not have local schools of management. The courses would be offered in German in Germany and Switzerland, in Spanish in the Latin American countries, and in English in the Far East.

Remuneration Policies

BBC's remuneration policy applies to personnel who are expatriated for one year or more. It seeks to assure a "reasonable standard of living" abroad ("Policy of the BBC Konzern on International Personnel Transfers" 1982). The company pays a foreign service allowance that adjusts for the cost-of-living and tax differentials. This allowance begins to decrease after the sixth year and is reduced to zero in the twelfth year. In addition, if the expatriate leaves his children in boarding schools in Switzerland, the company pays all the expenses.

For assignments to hardship locations, such as countries in the Communist bloc and certain countries in Africa, the company pays a hardship premium. Depending upon the local circumstances, the company may also provide guards and servants.

Success and Reasons for Success

Gamper reported that the incidence of expatriate failure at BBC is very low. Over the past seven years, he found one case in the first four years and three in the next three years. One person failed because he lacked the technical qualifications. Another failued because he was unable to adapt to the foreign country, in this case, Brazil. Although he learned Portugese and was well prepared technically for the position, he felt very isolated in the new country and, after a week there, refused to leave his room. (It should be noted that he grew up in a close-knit farm family with eleven brothers and sisters, and even during his university studies in Zurich he lived at home and spent evenings with his family.) A third expatriate failed because he developed an inflated notion of his importance abroad. For a single cocktail reception he gave at the best hotel in the foreign country, the individual spent 120,000 Swiss francs. This is reminiscent of the phenomenon Franco Mai of Olivetti described where the expatriate, by virtue of his status as the representative of a large foreign corporation, receives praise and adulation on a scale usually reserved for royalty.

Despite these isolated instances of poor performance abroad, the rate of expatriate failure at BBC is low. Gamper proffered four primary reasons for the success attained by BBC in this regard.

First, the Swiss show great interest in doing overseas work, often considering it something of an adventure. In Gamper's words, "If you consider [an overseas assignment] as a positive step, rather than just being sent, you are more willing to adapt to the new environment."

Second, the Swiss tend to be quite tolerant of others. This stems, in part, from the small size of their country and the absence of a colonial tradition. "We have never been masters in other countries like the British and the French," Gamper explained. "The former colonial powers may consider themselves as a different class and far superior to the local nationals. When we go to Nigeria, for example, we don't have the misconception that we are more intelligent than the Nigerians. I find that attitude very often among the American tourists and employees here; they feel that the American way is the right way. They don't consider that something can be done in five different ways, each with its own advantages and disadvantages. This ethnocentric attitude makes it difficult for them to adapt in a foreign environment. If you have the attitude that you preach others about the right things, you will not be accepted. Because we are a small country, we don't have the idea of becoming a leader. We don't impose a Swiss way of life. We take the attitude that since Brazil and Nigeria are bigger than we are, we are impressed to be there."

Third, being a small country, Switzerland can support only a limited number of companies in any given industry. In fact, in many cases, there may only be one employer for an industry. Thus, job mobility is low and commitment to companies is high.

Finally, BBC, like many other Swiss companies, makes allowance for less-than-average performance in the expatriate's initial period abroad. This relieves pressure to perform immediately on the job, which as noted earlier, may have dire consequences for the adaptation process in a foreign environment.

F. HOFFMAN – LA ROCHE & COMPANY

F. Hoffman – La Roche & Company (or La Roche for short) is another leading Swiss chemical manufacturer headquartered in Basel. It was founded in Switzerland in 1896, and in the same year it established its first foreign subsidiary in Germany. Now it has over forty companies in a corresponding number of different markets. In 1983 its consolidated worldwide sales reached 7.510 billion Swiss francs. The company is organized into six divisions: pharmaceuticals, vitamins and fine chemicals, perfumes and flavorings, diagnostics, instruments, and plant protection.

The information presented here was obtained from an in-depth interview with Guido Richterich, a member of the Executive Committee who has overall responsibility for human resource planning and management in the company.

Staffing Policies

In 1983 the company employed 45,852 people worldwide, 150 of whom served as expatriate staff. La Roche began its policy of expatriation some fifty years ago. Expatriates are currently assigned to operations in Latin America, Asia, and Africa. Expatriates are not used in the company's U.S. and European operations, where there are enough nationals with the necessary expertise to run the subsidiaries. Approximately 90 percent of La Roche's expatriates are Swiss.

La Roche has decreased its expatriate staff over the years. As the foreign subsidiaries have matured, parent-country nationals who were originally sent to establish the operations have been replaced by host-country nationals who have acquired the necessary skills and expertise to keep them running. La Roche's policy is to train and develop local talent and to use them where possible. In Japan, for example, the financial manager and the head of the pharmaceutical division are Japanese nationals. Only one expatriate manager remains in Brazil; all other top management positions are staffed by Brazilians or Europeans living in Brazil on their own accord. The latter are not employees expatriated by a particular company, but rather people who independently left home to seek their fortunes abroad. La Roche employs a number of such Swiss nationals in its Latin American operations. These people are not considered as expatriate personnel and are not entitled to expatriate benefits.

Since the late 1970s, La Roche has been using more third-country nationals in international assignments, primarily because an increasing number of employees in the company's foreign operations have actively sought and requested overseas experiences for career development purposes. Most of the third-country nationals come from the company's European operations. This is because the physical proximity and cultural similarity of the European operations to corporate headquarters are conducive to using such employees and because it is difficult to attract Americans to relocate to Basel.

Richterich indicated that many Americans are reluctant to work abroad for extended periods of time because they believe doing so may adversely affect their opportunities for future promotion in their company: "Once an American told me that if he were to accept an assignment to Basel for two to three years, it would not count toward his career in the United States." Richterich noted that, on numerous occasions, La Roche's headquarters had requested its U.S. subsidiary to nominate individuals interested in assignments to Basel. "We are not talking about transfers to other countries, just to Basel. Up till now, we have not received any request to come here." American nationals want an equivalent of their U.S. salary while they are in Basel, but fluctuations in the value of the U.S. dollar cause salary inequities with regard to their counterparts from Switzerland, France, and other countries. Furthermore, there appears to be a difference in philosophy toward expatriate assignments. "In Switzerland, Richterich explained, "we believe we cannot generalize in the sense of establishing written policies as they pertain to expatriation. Once abroad, the expatriate has to deal with the overseas situation in a very pragmatic way. For example, when we send a man to Nigeria, we cannot establish a policy first. He has to go there first and then approach it in a more pragmatic manner. It cannot be generalized." The American nationals apparently want a written policy before they go abroad. Given these differences in attitudes and philosophy toward expatriate assignments, American nationals are transferred only within the United States. While this may hinder their chances of promotion to the top of the hierarchy in corporate headquarters at Basel, it may not be an important consideration from the American perspective. The U.S. company is a large operation in itself, with 1,200 employees.

Those who aspire to top management positions in corporate headquarters must spend some time in Basel. At present, there are no foreign nationals on the Executive Committee in Basel. This derives, at least in part, from the fact that the use of third-country nationals in international assignments is a fairly recent practice. There is no conscientious attempt to exclude non-Swiss from Executive Committee appointments. Richterich believes that with the increasing use of third-country nationals in international assignments, ten or fifteen years hence, non-Swiss nationals may be promoted to the committee.

La Roche has two career paths, a domestic and an international track. Every year the company recruits approximately eight university graduates as management trainees (that is, they are not hired to fill specific positions). After their initial two-year training in Switzerland, half of these trainees are sent abroad and half remain in Basel.

The durations of expatriation vary depending upon the category of overseas assignments. For appointments at the chief executive officer level, the average duration is eleven years; for assignments in the functional head category, five years; and for assignments to hardship locations such as Nigeria, between three and four years. There is a divergence in opinion among members of corporate headquarters about the appropriate duration of expatriate assignments. Some argue that if a person performs well in a foreign country and is happy there he should not be recalled nor transferred. For this reason, those expatriates who are between the ages of fifty and fifty-two, and who have worked in their respective countries for ten years, may remain in the foreign country until they retire. The general managers of the operations in Italy and France, for example, have been there for eighteen and twenty-one years respectively. They are career expatriates. For career expatriates, the duration of overseas assignment is not stated explicitly in the contract.

Others at headquarters argue that expatriate assignments should be undertaken primarily for career development purposes. As such, expatriates should be rotated from one country to another or recalled to headquarters. People expatriated under this category are generally young. After gaining two to three years of experience in the domestic operation, they are assigned overseas for one to two years. In some of these assignments, they spend a year in one country and the second year in another. Trainees are assigned to work in a particular functional area, or area of specialization such as marketing or finance or production, in the foreign country.

At La Roche international experience is considered an integral part of overall career development. Individuals who aspire to senior management positions must have served abroad. In Richterich's words, "As a principle, we really say that to all our young people. We want them to learn how to behave in a foreign situation. Their management skills can also be better developed under those circumstances. That's why we believe that international experience is a necessity." For example, all members of the current Executive Committee have international experience. The youngest member of the committee, age forty-two, served for twelve years in La Roche's Japanese operation, ten years as general manager, and two years as a second-level manager. Another member served for five years in Argentina and an additional eight years in Brazil. "In general, the person should undertake two overseas assignments spanning ten to fifteen years," Richterich recommended.

Selection Criteria and Procedures

La Roche uses several criteria to identify people for overseas assignments. First and foremost is technical competence. Given the trend toward localization, the company must be convinced that the expatriate's professional qualifications are far superior to those of the host-country national's. Otherwise, his appointment cannot be justified. Second, the person must possess good managerial skills. Third, he must be willing to serve abroad. Fourth, he must be able to "adapt and integrate in the local ambience." Fifth, the person must be reliable and "should not leave behind any problems in Switzerland." In other words, the company wants to be certain that the person is genuinely interested in undertaking an overseas assignment for the right reasons. Richterich explained, "We are skeptical if a person has lots of debts or is recently divorced, and therefore just wants to leave Switzerland." While the company does not administer tests to gauge these attributes, it does solicit the opinions of four or five line managers, including the personnel manager, who are familiar with the person's day-to-day behavior. Sixth, the candidate must have language proficiency if he is assigned to a European country; this requirement is waived for assignments to countries, such as Japan, with more exotic languages. Finally, the status of children's education comes into play. Since most Swiss are averse to leaving their children in boarding schools, the company checks whether appropriate schooling is available in the foreign country. If the children are currently enrolled in a German school, for example, La Roche finds a similar facility in the destination country before expatriating the employee.

Training Programs

La Roche offers several types of training programs to prepare their expatriates for living and working abroad. These are described below.

Language Training.   The company provides in-house training programs in English, French, Spanish, Italian, and German. The latter course is designed for international transferees assigned to positions in Basel. In general, La Roche believes that English, as the *lingua franca* of international commerce, is adequate for most foreign assignments. In Richterich's words, "Without English, nobody will have a chance."

Most Swiss do not have problems with the European languages because they are taught several languages in school. Every university graduate speaks German and French in addition to English. Some also speak Spanish and Italian. If the person is to assume a senior management position in a Spanish-speaking country, he receives intensive training because proficiency in the language is deemed essential for effective performance at that level. The expatriate who was appointed chief executive officer in Ecuador underwent a two-month intensive Spanish language program in Madrid, which his wife also attended. The company paid all expenses associated with this language-immersion course.

The company believes that it is too complicated for the expatriate to master exotic languages such as Japanese or Korean. Recounting his own experience in Korea, Richterich noted, "I learned a little bit of Korean primarily for demonstration purposes, that is, to show the local people that I was interested in their culture. We would never have been able to master the business language. The member of our Executive Committee who has spent twelve years in Japan understands Japanese, but he cannot write it. Learning Japanese can be done as a hobby only. We cannot expect the expatriate to be thoroughly fluent in it, however." If expatriates were assigned to low-level positions in these countries, it would be necessary for them to learn the language. Every year the Nestle corporation, for example, hires five or six young Swiss college graduates to sell coffee in Japan and requires them to learn Japanese. Since most of La Roche's assignments to Japan are at the senior management level, however, where the medium of communication is English, knowledge of Japanese is deemed unnecessary.

Cross-cultural Training.   The company does not provide a formal cross-cultural program to prepare its expatriates for living and working abroad, but it does provide books and other materials pertaining to the history and customs of the foreign country. "There is no need for us to make people aware of the necessity to prepare themselves for such a job," Richterich explained. "As soon as a man knows he is being assigned to a foreign coutnry, he starts learning about the country. In short, most of our people are really willing to serve abroad. In my travels abroad, I find that Americans tend to aggregate too much in their own circles. While our expatriates may join special clubs, in general, we recommend that our people integrate with the local community and try to live according to the local lifestyle. Normally our people are interested in so doing. I think that is the best way to gain acceptance by the local people."

Richterich acknowledged that with the rising number of dual-career families, La Roche has to contend with the issue of persuading expatriates' wives to go abroad. Beginning in 1984, on two occasions, La Roche offered wives the opportunity to visit the foreign country "to convince them that they can make a good living abroad. In both cases, it worked."

Management Training.   While management training programs are not specifically associated with expatriation, they are described briefly here, since international experience is an integral part of overall career development at La Roche. The main component of La Roche's management development programs is a three-week course designed for those identified as possessing high potential for senior management positions. The purpose of this program is to allow maximum interaction of participants with members of the Executive Committee and to hone their management skills to meet changes necessitated by the new sociological and economic developments at home and abroad. In addition, the company sponsors several short in-house programs aimed at broadening the person's understanding in the areas of managing people, decisionmaking, cost analysis, project management, planning, and so on.

For external programs, La Roche utilizes the facilities of international management schools, such as IMEDE, to familiarize its employees with the international environment. All expatriates attend at least one course at IMEDE before going abroad.

Remuneration Policies

Where possible, expatriates are paid local salaries. In practice, however, the company usually pays an allowance to adjust for the cost-of-living differential abroad. As an inducement to serve in countries such as Indonesia and Nigeria, the company pays a hardship premium.

Repatriation

Repatriation is generally not a problem at La Roche because many people who accept international assignments are career expatriates. "In our opinion," Richterich said, "those who leave Switzerland and have embarked on an international career are not interested in coming home because the opportunities abroad are good. For example, a forty-year old man can be head of the pharmaceutical division in Indonesia—the pay is good and the person assumes lots of responsibilities. Back here, he is just one of hundreds. Normally, they don't come back except for family reasons or when they are offered very good positions here. If we force them to come back, they will be unhappy. They will ask whether we can promise to send them overseas in two years' time. From our standpoint, that is a greater problem." This echoes the sentiment expressed by Franco Mai of Olivetti.

Richterich projected that this situation may change in the future because of new organizational developments. In the past, most people served one assignment at the middle management level before being promoted to the position of general manager. Due to the stabilization of the company's growth (i.e., since operations have already been established in most world markets), the rate of promotion will be slower in the future. Consequently, an increasing number of people will have to undertake two or three assignments at the same level, either in the same country or in a different one, before being promoted to the next higher level of management. "This may cause problems because everybody expects to be promoted. Even if they remain at the same level, they hope to be transferred to a bigger foreign operation. Because of this new development, we will have more people in headquarters who are between assignments." Richterich hopes to make this new situation benefit both corporate headquarters and the expatriates. In the past, those at headquarters believed that expatriates spent too little time in corporate headquarters between assignments to become fully acquainted with events at home. With a longer time span between overseas assignments, this problem can be rectified. Expatriates can "become more a part of the family here—they can be more in touch with the problems we are faced with here." Expatriates can also benefit from the longer time spent in headquarters by atending courses to develop further their managerial and technical skills.

Success and Reasons for Success

Richterich reported, "We do not have one expatriate who is locally a failure." While some expatriates requested to be transferred home for family reasons, such as the inability of the wife or children to adjust to the local climate, there was no instance where the person returned before his contract was over. Richterich proffered several reasons for the low rate of expatriate failure at La Roche.

First was the expatriates' genuine desire to serve abroad. As noted earlier, given the good salary and larger responsibility associated with overseas positions, most expatriates are truly interested in working abroad. In fact, some are reluctant to return home.

Second, Richterich cited the Swiss tradition of emigration abroad. Since Switzerland is a small country, it is common for at least one family member to have left home to make his fortune elsewhere. This is similar to the situation in the United Kingdom and Italy. Thus, many Swiss view an overseas assignment as an attractive means of advancing their career and livelihood, and they make every effort to adapt to the foreign environment. Americans, on the other hand, generally seek the amenities of home duplicated in a foreign land. In other words, they want to "create a piece of America wherever they go." According to Richterich, because of the smallness of their country, the Swiss "cannot try to create a Swiss community abroad. Consequently, from the beginning, we are forced to make friends and mix with other nationalities, whether they be local nationals or other foreigners." Echoing the sentiments expressed by an executive of another Swiss MNC he said, "We don't expect people to take care of us abroad. Therefore, we have to do our best to adjust to the local surroundings." Richterich hypothesized that the army experience common to all Swiss men may also influence their attitude toward survival and tolerance of hardship. "We all start as soldiers. We all start at the same level and undergo the same basic training. There is no elite, so to speak. We are accustomed to participating in unpleasant situations. So maybe there is a carryover from our army days—most Swiss are prepared to bear with unpleasant situations." Even in Karachi, Pakistan, where the living conditions are harsh, some La Roche expatriates have lived for over five years and are "quite happy." Richterich further hypothesized that the Swiss emphasis on egalitarianism is also reflected in their management style. "There is not that much of an elitism. This [style of management] meets with better reception elsewhere."

A third reason for the low rate of expatriate failure may be attributed to the fact that the duration of an assignment is not stated at the time of expatriation. Expatriates do not know when, or even whether, they will be recalled. In Richterich's words, "There may be no ticket home. Therefore, they have to blend into the local system." This serves as a powerful incentive for the person to adapt to the local conditions. If he were told that he was to remain in the foreign country for three years only, he might have no desire to learn and adjust to the local society. Because of the temporary nature of the assignment "he doesn't care whether he is accepted."

Finally, since international experience is an integral part of overall career development at La Roche, expatriates have good reason to make a success of their foreign assignments. The rate of job turnover at La Roche is very low. In fact, the company almost has a system of lifetime employment similar to that of Japanese MNCs (Tung 1984a). Dr. Richterich was cognizant that this low job turnover may be attributed to the fact that La Roche experienced substantial growth in the past when it could offer fast rates of promotion and good opportunities for all of its employees. Once the company's growth stabilizes, the rate of job turnover may increase. While this may be true, given the small size of Switzerland and the limited number of industries and companies each industry can support, it is doubtful that the turnover rate will approach the magnitude prevalent in the United States.

6 GERMAN MULTINATIONALS

This chapter examines the international human resource management practice at a large German multinational, Siemens AG. The Siemens Group is a leading international manufacturer of electrical and electronic products and systems. It is organized into six business groups and five corporate divisions. The six business groups are components, power engineering and automation, electrical installations, communication and information systems, medical engineering, and telecommunication networks and security systems. The five corporate divisions are corporate business administration, corporate finance, corporate personnel, corporate technology, and corporate sales and marketing.

The Siemens Group is one of the world's six largest companies in the electrical and electronic industry. In 1982–83, group sales totaled 39,471 Deutsch marks. Group turnover is around $16 to $17 billion per annum, 44 percent of which is derived from the Federal Republic of Germany, 24 percent from the rest of Europe, 11 percent from Asia and Australia, 9 percent from North America, and 6 percent each from Latin America and Africa. Siemens has 108 subsidiaries in twenty-six countries and equity interest of up to 50 percent in fifty-five manufacturing facilities in another thirty countries.

The group employs 320,000 people worldwide, 45 percent of whom belong to the sales organization. The geographic distribution of Siemens workforce is as follows: 220,00 in Germany, 50,000 in other countries in Europe, 15,300 in Latin America, 14,400 in North America, 14,000 in Asia and Australia, and 6,900 in Africa.

The information presented here was obtained through in-depth interviews with Klaus Kramer, director of central personnel; Werner Eichenlaub, director of personnel; and Raimund Gmeiner, a member of central personnel. These three men have responsibility for all personnel issues in the sales group, the largest part of Siemens organization, and all international assignments, including transfers to and from Germany.

Staffing Policies

In 1984 the group employed 885 expatriates, 1 percent of whom were third-country nationals. At Siemens, the classification of personnel into parent-, host- and third-country nationals is not determined by citizenship but by the base country from which the person is transferred. For example, a Dutch national employed in Germany and then transferred to the United States is considered a parent-country national, not a third-country national. If citizenship were used as the basis for categorization, then the percentage of third-country nationals among the total expatriate staff would increase significantly. Most third-country nationals at Siemens come from other European countries. The rationale for their use is that they are deemed the best people for the jobs.

The number of expatriates at Siemens has remained relatively constant over the past twenty years, although the percentage of expatriates has been halved. The geographic distribution of country of assignments is as follows: 24.9 percent in Europe, 28.6 percent in Asia and Australia, 30.8 percent in the Americas, and 15.7 percent in Africa. Expatriates assume positions in various functional areas at all levels. Approximately 26.4 percent assume top management positions, 51.7 percent work at the middle management level, and 21.9 percent are engaged in nonexempt functions. The latter are specialist roles to transfer technology and to facilitate the introduction of new production processes and services. In the field of medical engineering, for example, expatriates serve specialist functions in the maintenance of machinery and the provision of other types of services.

Since the mid 1970s, Siemens' policy has been to use expatriates only when there are no qualified local nationals to fill the positions. This policy of localization has been largely successful. In Brazil, for example, 57 percent of upper management positions were staffed by parent- and third-country nationals in 1976. By 1983 that number had dropped to 24 percent. At the middle management level, the use of expatriate staff decreased from 29 percent in 1976 to 11 percent in 1983. Similar statistics prevail for Colombia and India. In Colombia, in 1976, all upper management positions were occupied by expatriates but by 1983, 37 percent were assumed by host-country nationals; host-country nationals staffed only 75 percent of the middle management positions in 1976, compared with 84 percent in 1983. In India, 58 percent of upper management positions were occupied by host-country nationals in 1976, compared with 88 percent in 1983. At the middle management level, expatriates held 26 percent of the positions in 1976, compared with only 4 percent in 1983. Statistics for other parts of the world are as follows: in Europe (excluding Germany), of the 393 upper management and 2,490 middle management positions, only 64 and 100, respectively, are occupied by expatriates. For positions outside Europe, only 83 of the 258 senior management positions and 122 of the 1,404 middle management positions are occupied by expatriate personnel.

The average duration of an overseas assignment is from two to three years for nonexempt functions and a minimum of five to six years for positions in the chief executive officer and managing director categories. The duration of assignment to locations with harsh living conditions is generally shorter. For example, the maximum transfer period to the Gulf States and Africa (except for South Africa) is three years. Upon completion of their assignments abroad, most expatriates return to headquarters. The home department initiating the international transfer contract guarantees reemployment of expatriates upon completion of their overseas assignments. A minority of expatriates become career expatriates. According to Kramer, "Many people who have been abroad like to serve overseas again."

There are increasingly more international transfers to Germany for training purposes. In 1983-84, for example, there were 135 transferees from Africa to Germany, compared with 46 expatriates from Germany to Africa; 231 transferees from Latin America, compared with 39 expatriates from Germany: and 139 transferees from Asia to Germany, compared with 51 expatriates to Asia. Transferees come from one of two categories of personnel: (1) all levels of managers, including members of senior management, and (2) young professionals from engineering, sales, and administration, who demonstrate high potential for future advancement within their respective companies. These young professionals have between two and four years of experience with the local company. The duration of an international transfer averages from two to three years. Transferees are attached to a line function in one of the six business groups, and their technical training is acquired primarily on the job. In addition, transferees undergo language and intercultural training.

Selection Criteria and Procedures

Siemens adopts several criteria to assess a person's suitability for an international assignment. First and foremost is technical competence.

Second is willingness to work abroad. Third is language proficiency. Like at most European multinationals, this criterion applies to the major European languages only, namely, English, French, and Spanish. Knowledge of exotic languages, such as Arabic, Chinese, and Japanese, is not required. Fourth is the person's ability to adjust to a foreign country. Siemens does not use tests to gauge this dimension; rather it is done in conjunction with the annual assessment of performance and potential. Since most expatriates assume managerial positions abroad, they generally have been with the company for many years and their adaptability can be accurately assessed on past performance. Finally is the willingness of the spouse to live abroad. For assignments at the upper and middle management levels, the spouse's opinion is solicited. For technical positions, the spouses's preferences may not be considered in the selection decision.

If an employee turns down an overseas assignment for valid reasons, it generally does not adversely affect his opportunities for advancement. The company recognizes that there are increasing problems associated with dual-career couples. In these situations, rather than paying the spouse a lump sum as an incentive to work overseas, Siemens assists her in finding a suitable position abroad.

While international experience is considered an important requisite for promotion to top management, not all members of senior management have worked abroad. Both Eichenlaub and Gmeiner attributed this to the large size of Siemens' domestic operation. At other European MNCs with large overseas subsidiaries and fairly small domestic operations, there is ample opportunity for parent-country nationals to assume positions abroad. At Siemens, because two-thirds of its workforce is employed in Germany, and because it has a strong policy of localization, providing international experience to all candidates for top management positions is very difficult logistically. In addition, the various functional divisions provide differing amounts of international experience. In the sales organization, many people have worked abroad. For example, Kramer has lived overseas for twelve years. In the research and development organization, in contrast, the opportunities for overseas work are very limited.

Training Programs

All expatriates are exposed to four blocks of training programs to prepare them for international assignments. These programs are provided concurrently, not sequentially.

Technical Training.   This program does not stress the teaching of technical skills because all candidates are assessed as technically competent before being selected. Rather, the emphasis of this module is to introduce the candidate to partners and associates abroad, people with whom he will work overseas. The candidate also acquires information about additional products he will represent abroad. This training averages from two to three weeks.

Language Training.   Siemens invests heavily in language programs. Besides courses in English, French, Spanish, and Portugese, the company has initiated training in Japanese, Chinese, and Arabic. Language training is begun as soon as the selection decision is made. The training usually entails two to three hours of private lessons two or three times a week for a period of two months. In most cases this two-month training is followed by a one-month intensive program held in a country where the language is spoken. For English-language training, the person is sent to the United Kingdom. The expatriate continues to receive language training after he arrives in the destination country. At this stage, the training can take the form of a crash course or additional private lessons conducted over several months. In most cases, spouses are included in the language training program.

Cross-cultural Training.   Siemens sends its people to the Center for International Briefing, Farnham Castle (U.K.) and the Carl-Duisberg Center and Evangelische Akademie in Bad Boll (West Germany). When possible, the expatriates' wives attend the program as well.

Environmental Briefing.   Given its extensive history of overseas operation, Siemens has accumulated much information about foreign countries which it provides to expatriates and their families. Most of the environmental briefing is conducted in-house.

Management Training.   In addition to these four blocks of training that are specific to expatriation, Siemens provides management programs at various levels. At the lower management level, there is a one-week course entitled ''Basic Management Seminar,'' which offers training in management styles and methods, career planning, and staff evaluation. This program is attended by all employees deemed capable of attaining at least middle management positions. A second level of training is designed to update the knowledge of middle management personnel and to prepare them for the responsibilities of higher management. The third level of training is a three-week program attended by all middle managers who are about to be promoted to senior management.

Beyond these three levels of programs, there are additional seminars related to specific organizational functions, such as public speaking, managing large numbers of employees, strategic planning, and managing MNCs in a changing political environment. These programs are offered either in-house or by external agencies and are attended by members of top management.

Remuneration Policies

Unlike at most multinationals, expatriates at Siemens are paid according to the local wage scales, that is, the expatriate's income is comparable to that of a local national who occupies a position at the same level and who has attained the same level of performance. In addition, the company pays all expenses associated with the transfer, such as an allowance for housing, medical expenses, and children's schooling. It also pays toward the expatriate's pension and medical insurance plans at home.

For assignments to countries with lower local salaries, a financial incentive is offered, including free housing, bonus payments, and other fringe benefits. For assignments to hardship locations, a premium is paid. According to Gmeiner, for most people who accept assignments to hardship locations, the principal incentive is not financial but related to career advancement. "We try to make it rewarding for the person, as far as his career within the company is concerned."

Eichenlaub conceded that, in recent years, the company has had to increase its incentive package. Some further perquisites the company hopes to provide are luxurious free housing, company cars, club memberships, and so on.

Success and Reasons for Success

According to Gmeiner, the incidence of expatriate failure at Siemens is less than one case a year. None of the failures can be attributed to lack of technical ability; rather they stem from health reasons or family situations, including the wife's inability to adjust to the foreign way of life and/or problems with the children's schooling. The region of the world that poses the greatest difficulty for expatriates is Africa because of climate, health, and isolation considerations.

Several reasons were given for the low rate of expatriate failure at Siemens.

First, Siemens has nearly a century of experience in operating abroad. So its oveseas plants are well established. "All the facilities overseas are similar to that in Germany" explained Kramer. "In places where we have the large power stations, we build company towns with schools, and so on." Under these circumstances, expatriates are not required to venture into new territory. This reduces the tension often associated with overseas relocation.

Second, Siemens has a strong corporate culture. According to Eichenlaub, "The company culture is more or less similar in all our operations, so it does not make much difference whether the person is in Germany, Brazil, or India." This culture is inculcated in the local nationals through their training in corporate headquarters. Every year, approximately one thousand foreign nationals are brought to Germany for training. Thus, local companies are thoroughly familiar with corporate philosophy, practices, and systems. "Over the years, we have implemented our culture in the companies abroad. This is perhaps the main reason for the low failure rate."

Third, through careful selection of candidates for international assignments, Siemens reduces the possibility of expatriating those who may fail. Since most candidates have been with the company for a long time, there has been ample opportunity to assess their suitability for overseas positions.

Fourth, like their British counterparts, many of the German MNCs were established during the heyday of European imperialism, and the legacy of the empire remains. Kramer acknowledged that "there is a bit of [the empire spirit] in us too." This helps account for the Germans' willingness to work abroad.

Fifth, Siemens makes allowance for less-than-average performance during the initial period abroad. Expatriates assigned to business and administrative functions are given an adjustment period of three to four months. Those in sales and engineering can become operational in a few months if they have facility in the local language; otherwise, it takes almost a year. While people who are assigned to chief executive officer and managing director positions can perform almost immediately, the company recognizes that it will take them one to two years to develop all the necessary external contacts.

Finally, the low rate of employee turnover—around 3.5 percent per annum—due to low job mobility tends to engender a greater commitment and loyalty among the employees. This resembles the situation in Japanese MNCs where employees are prepared to undertake temporary inconveniences called for in a job because of the overall advantages of lifetime employment.

7 TRANSNATIONAL CORPORATIONS

This chapter examines the international human resource management practices at two transnational corporations. Following Dymsza's definition (1972), a transnational corporation is a multinational firm owned by peoples of different nationalities with two or more parent headquarters. The two transnational corporations discussed here are Unilever and another company disguised as the LMN Group, in accordance with its desire to remain anonymous.

The information on Unilever was obtained through an in-depth interview with A.J.P. Vineall, deputy head of personnel. The information on the LMN Group was obtained through interviews with two managers of the Central Personnel unit in the parent corporation.

Staffing Policies

Unilever has two parent companies, one British and the other Dutch. Its history of expatriation dates back to the turn of the century. Presently, the company employs 300,000 employees worldwide, 1,200 of whom serve as expatriate staff. The regional distribution of its expatriates is almost equally divided between the advanced nations and the less-developed countries. Specifically, about 500 expatriates are located in Europe; 40 are in North America; and the remainder are scattered over the globe mostly in third-world nations but also in Australia and South Africa. While the total number of expatriates has decreased significantly over the past three decades, Vineall indicated that it will stabilize at the present level for two primary reasons. One, Unilever's continuing expansion into new areas of business and new product groups abroad necessitates the transfer of technology from parent headquarters to overseas subsidiaries. Parent-country nationals are generally used for the transfer of technology. Two, Unilever people with high potential for senior management will be sent abroad for management development purposes, specifically, to give them an international perspective.

While expatriates typically occupy positions at the top and middle management levels, they do not monopolize such positions. In fact, on average, only 5 to 6 percent of the top management positions in Europe and approximately 20 percent of the senior management positions in third-world countries are staffed by expatriates, while 3 and 6 percent of the middle management positions are staffed by expatriates in Europe and third-world countries, respectively.

The 1,200 expatriate staff figure includes third-country nationals. The reasons for LMN's rather extensive use of third-country nationals are twofold. First, many of Unilever's smaller overseas operations may have many talented people whose skills and expertise may be demanded elsewhere. Denmark, for example, has surplus talent. Because of its small size, the Danish subsidiary can offer only limited prospects for advancement locally. In Vineall's words, "If you've got two or three very capable Danes, and they are all the same age, there is no career opportunity for some, that is, you can't make them all the boss. So they are quite pleased to move overseas." Second, a foreign assignment usually precedes a promotion to the position of chairman or chief executive officer of a local company. While it cannot be categorically said that a person without international experience cannot be promoted to the parent boards, "we get very close to that," said Vineall. Given the multinational nature of Unilever's operations, third-country nationals (i.e., non-Briton and non-Dutch) can also be appointed to the boards of the parent companies. Nationalities represented on present and past boards include Indian, Australian, German, and Norwegian.

At Unilever the duration of an expatriate assignment averages from two and one-half to three years. Since expatriate assignments are an integral part of a manager's overall career development, most high achievers serve one or two tours of duty abroad. Only a few employees spend substantial proportions of their careers abroad.

The LMN Group also has two European parent companies. To protect its identity, the nationalities of these companies will not be disclosed. There are four service centers, two in each parent country. The LMN Group is a conglomeration of some five hundred independent companies with shareholding relationships in various businesses. The group employs approximately 170,000 people, 5,000 of whom are located in the two parent companies. Each LMN Group employee has two "parents": a parent company to which he belongs contractually and a parent function with which he is affiliated, such as marketing or finance. Most people join LMN at a local operating company. For example, most of its German employees are recruited by the German operating company. However, "the core of the LMN Group's culture is that anybody who is going to reach a management team will have worked outside of his own operating company at some stage," to quote one of the managers. Similarly, each management team in the parent and local operating companies generally has a member who is a foreign national on assignment from another operating company. This person may come from any functional area. These practices are designed to ensure an international perspective in the decisionmaking and operations of both the parent organizations and the local companies. One manager interviewed noted that his unit, for example, is comprised of people of seventeen different nationalities. Each person is an expert in his respective field and has been assigned to the parent organization to be "broadened internationally." At the LMN Group, expatriate assignments are viewed as an integral part of management development.

In the past, most international transfers were from the parent organizations to the local operating companies. Now, the pattern has reversed. Local nationals with potential for promotion beyond certain positions (according to a standardized Hay evaluation procedure) are sent to one of the parent organizations for broader exposure to corporate operations. These people generally have more than ten years of experience with the local company.

In the past, parent-country nationals undertook expatriate assignments almost immediately upon joining the company and began at fairly low-level positions abroad. Some of them went on to become career expatriates. Career expatriates are now being phased out. Employees with potential for management positions now retain a home-country base and generally serve two or three assignments abroad in the course of their career with the LMN Group. At present, new recruits of the parent organizations can expect two or three of their first five assignments to be outside of their respective home countries. Beyond that, assignments are made primarily on the basis of whether the person intends to develop into a generalist or specialist.

Expatriate assignments are generally made in one of three situations. One, an expatriate may be used to fill a managerial void in a foreign location. If a gap in management succession occurs in a local operating company, a parent- or third-country national may be sent in, at least temporarily, until a host-country national is ready to assume the position. Two, an expatriate may be used to staff an expert function, such as retail planning or marketing. In this situation, the expatriate fills the position and also trains a local successor. Three, expatriation may occur for career development reasons. The parent organization may request a local operating company temporarily to take in some of its promising young employees to give them some international experience. According to one manager at the LMN Group, "The people who staff the more responsible positions in the service companies must have recent frontline experience, otherwise they will not have an understanding of world market conditions." Quid pro quo, the parent organization accepts an equal number of senior managers from the local operating company for management development, or "broadening," at headquarters.

At the LMN Group the average duration of an overseas assignment is from three to four years, extended from the previous term of two to three years. The reasons for this extension are threefold. One, it is a means of reducing the high cost associated with frequent transfers. Two, it provides continuity in relations in an operating company. Tung (1984a) found that Japanese companies often complain about the rapid rotation of American personnel, rendering it difficult to establish the trust that is fundamental to business relationships in Japan. Three, it provides the expatriate adequate time to perform his job well.

The LMN Group is organized into several geographic regions: Europe, East (Southeast Asia and Australia), West (Central America, South America, and the Caribbean), North America, the Middle East, and Africa. The heads of these regional groups are stationed at the parent corporations. Every year the central personnel units at the parent organizations meet with senior management from the major operating companies to discuss staffing issues. At these meetings, the chief executive officers of the local operating companies present projections of their staffing needs and proposals for meeting these needs. Sometimes an exchange is arranged on the spot. The smaller operating companies generally hold analogous discussions once every two years. In addition, members of personnel from each regional group in the parent companies travel to the operating companies in their respective jurisdictions to acquire an overall perspective of managerial needs.

The international exchanges arranged through these staff meetings may be inter- or intra-regional. One manger of the LMN Group commented, "People will not be put in an area they are familiar with. For broadening purposes, they will be put in a different area to acquire skills which are relatable, but which are not directly related to their home territory. At the end of the day, the general manager or chief executive or marketing director of an operating company is serving LMN worldwide—his customers are worldwide, so he has got to have this international perspective of the business." Because LMN expects its managers to be familiar with its operations in both the advanced and the less developed countries, its employees are willing to accept assignments to the less-developed countries.

Selection Criteria and Procedures

Unilever adopts two major criteria in selecting people for overseas assignments. First and foremost is technical competence: the job must be done, and the expatriate "won't have any hope of acceptance in the host country unless he is visibly and perceptibly better than the people they have there," to quote Vineall. In fact, most host governments will not issue work permits to foreigners when local nationals can fill the job openings. Second is suitability to engage in work abroad, determined by the candidate's interest in an overseas assignment, flexibility in new environmental settings, and resilience to the pressures and strains of overseas work. The company does not gauge the spouse's suitability but does take into consideration any available information about the spouse in determining the candidate's suitability.

While Unilever tries to consider extenuating circumstances that may preclude a person from accepting an overseas assignment at a particular time, it cannot always accommodate specific requests because, in the final analysis, a job needs to be done overseas. Vineall indicated that high achievers at Unilever are explicitly told that if they want to rise to the top of the organization or get "even moderately near it," they will be required to work overseas at some point. Given the global nature of Unilever's business, "you can't have people in important jobs at the top who have not been through the experience of working in someone else's country." Most people who occupy senior management positions have been abroad at least once. In fact, many have served two tours of duty overseas.

At the LMN Group several criteria are used in selecting people for cross-country postings: technical competence, linguistic abilities (critical to successful performance abroad), good interactive skills (i.e., the ability to relate to people of other cultures), and willingness to serve abroad. The latter dimension is gauged in the annual evaluation. As one manager explained, "You don't want to put people under impossible constraints. An expatriate failure is extremely expensive, not only in terms of money, but also because you wreck the man."

In general, the company can make a fairly accurate assessment of a person's interactive skills. People from the various regions meet at regular intervals; hence, they know each other fairly well. As noted earlier, the Central Postings Unit and the regional heads visit their subsidiaries frequently, so they either know the individuals under consideration personally or know someone whose judgment of the candidates they can trust. In addition, most of the company's management training programs are attended by people of different nationalities and from different countries, which facilitates the development of interactive and communication skills among nationals of various countries. In assignments undertaken primarily for career development purposes, the Central Postings Unit arranges for the chief executive or a member of senior management from the local operating company to interview the candidate when the former visits the parent organization. If this meeting cannot be scheduled, the regional manager in the parent company interviews the candidate. Finally, LMN's policy of including a foreign national in each management team allows employees without prior overseas experience to work alongside foreign nationals. This in turn allows the personnel unit to gauge his relational skills. While the LMN Group does not formally assess a spouse's suitability for living overseas, according to a manager, "Within the framework of LMN's corporate culture, most people's wives are known to others in the normal course of the business. . . . We are sensitive to what the personnel job is about. There are many things one hears that are never put down on paper." Given the lifetime employment practice and the strong corporate culture at the LMN Group the personnel units are familiar with their employees' family situations. In this way, LMN is similar to Japanese multinationals (Tung 1984a).

If an employee refuses an overseas assignment, it will have a negative effect on his subsequent career advancement in that he will not be qualified for certain jobs. While LMN, like other multinationals, understands that its employees may be less mobile at some times than at others, "to not go out at all will have a negative impact. In a major international company, you have to be mobile," explained one manager.

Training Programs

Unilever provides several types of training programs to prepare its expatriates for overseas assignments. These include language training, technical training, cultural orientation, and management training.

Language Training.   The candidate and spouse undergo a one-week intensive language training program. The company uses outside facilities, such as Berlitz, when feasible; otherwise, private tutoring may be arranged. For this reason, the personnel group keeps an inventory of people who can provide conversational lessons.

Technical Training.   The kind of technical training provided depends upon the job to be performed abroad. Since it is rare to find a person who has the exact skills and knowledge required for the overseas vacancy, the company generally tailors the training to the specific expatriate and job. For example, if the person's experience is in detergent manufacturing and he will have to assume responsibility for both detergent and toothpaste manufacturing abroad, Unilever will arrange for him to visit a toothpaste manufacturing plant to learn the specifics of that business.

Cultural Orientation.   Unilever utilizes the week-long cross-cultural program offered by the Center for International Briefing, Farnham Castle. The company believes it is absolutely essential for expatriates to understand and accept cultural differences and considers the center's program an excellent introduction to fostering such tolerance. "Of course, you can't do it in a week, but you can at least dent people's overconfidence that they understand by saying that it is different overseas, and you are not going to change it because it will go on being different."

Management Training.   Like at most multinationals, management training at Unilever is not specifically tied to an overseas assignment; rather, it is designed for all employees with potential for higher management. Most of the programs are conducted in-house, although the company also uses outside facilities at INSEAD, IMEDE, the London Business School, and several U.S. business schools.

The LMN Group also provides language training, technical training, cultural orientation, and management training. For assignments to exotic countries where it is critical to speak the local language, the expatriate is given a three-month intensive linguistic program. LMN has large in-house training centers in both parent countries, which offer most of the technical and management training programs.

Remuneration Policies

Unilever gives its expatriate allowances for extra expenses incurred in living abroad. In general, an expatriate can enjoy at least the same standard of living he is accustomed to at home. Instead of paying a hardship premium for an assignment to a location with harsh living conditions, Unilever gives a "terminal bonus"—a percentage of gross salary for every year served in that country. A higher terminal bonus is paid at the end of an assignment to a less desirable location.

The LMN Group's remuneration package is composed of several elements: spending, discretionary savings, expatriate inducement (which varies according to the desirability of the location), housing, and tax differential. Every expatriate receives a pension-based salary indexed to his job level at home.

Repatriation

The head of personnel in the expatriate's home country and Vineall's office share the joint responsibility of supervising the career path of the expatriate while he is overseas. Vineall indicated that a major reason for the relatively short duration of overseas assignments at Unilever is to avoid possible repatriation problems. If the assignment abroad were prolonged, the expatriate is given a clear indication of the duration and what awaits him upon reentry. According to Vineall, repatriation may be the most difficult aspect of an international transfer. "The thing which gives expatriate experience a bad reputation faster than anything else is poor reabsorption or reintegration back into the mainstream in the home country," he explained. "The money issue can be coped with; teaching them the language can also be dealt with—you can teach them all those things. But you won't win even if you do all that right, if they see that the last person who came back was worse off than when he left. Every time there is a casualty, it gets magnified more than a hundredfold. Like everything in life, everybody knows about the casualty and they forget about all the ones that were successful. You do damage most quickly by bad onward career progression than anything else.'' While such instances of negative career progression are rare, Vineall acknowledged that when they occur, they are ''widely known.''

In the LMN Group, one manager indicated that there can be problems of reabsorption if too many people were expatriated from a single country and all returned at the same time. ''At times, there are redundancies going on—people do feel vulnerable.'' However, since most assignments are now undertaken for career development purposes, the new generation of expatriates is selected from the pool of high achievers. They can often be promoted upon return, thus obviating repatriation problems that occur with less competent employees. People going out on non-international contracts (i.e., not as permanent expatriates) are guaranteed reentry. Moreover, the parent function charged with overseeing each employee's progression, acts as an in-house facilitator for smooth repatriation.

Repatriation problems occur primarily among career expatriates. The pressure for localization in most countries has necessitated their repatriation. Particularly for employees who are relatively advanced in years, reabsorption may be difficult. LMN generally offers them the option of early retirement. Since career expatriates are now being phased out, these problems will eventually subside.

Success and Reasons for Success

Only 1 percent of Unilever's expatriates actually fail on the job and must be repatriated. Approximately 10 percent of the assignments prove disappointing to the company. In these cases, Unilever sees that the overseas job ''has done very little to develop him as a person. It may even have done the reverse.'' If the problem stems from the family's poor adjustment, Unilever tries to defuse the situation by bringing the spouse back earlier or shortening the duration of the assignment. As Vineall observed, ''We try not to see it as a win-lose/succeed-fail dichotomy. Occasionally it is like that. But in general we try to accommodate the preferences of the people and they, in turn, try to do the right thing by the business.''

The cases of maladjustment are not confined to a particular country or region but are fairly evenly distributed across geographic locations. The greatest difficulties occur in countries with harsh physical environments or very marked cultural differences. Vineall cites Japan as an example of a country in the latter category. "The thing that frightens [expatriates], and they don't realize it until they get there, is that you can't even read the signs. . . . If you are going to some remote village on the Congo, everybody expects it to be strange. They have been prepared for it and they expect it." Expatriates' expectations of Japan, however, may be misguided. If they equate modernization with Westernization, and hence expect a country very similar to home, they will be disappointed and frustrated by the cultural differences.

When asked to give some reasons for the relatively low rate of actual expatriate failure, Vineall cited the following factors.

First, Unilever makes allowances for less-than-average performance in the initial adjustment period abroad. However, the company generally sends abroad those who can and do settle quickly.

Second, because of the smaller size of their countries, Europeans generally "are more aware that there are other countries with other ways of living than is the average American." Vineall pointed out that, Americans "live in a huge country with something approaching a common culture from coast to coast, with a population the size of the whole fourteen countries of West Europe, all with one president and one language." In Europe, however, people "grow up realizing that there are different cultures. . . . You can't go far without getting into another culture. So it isn't strange, it isn't just a lot of funny people who are speaking your language badly when they go abroad. They have been used to those people all their lives."

Third, Unilever has developed a comprehensive network to assist its expatriates. In every country of foreign operation, there is a contact manager who meets all the incoming and outgoing expatriates. This manager is knowledgeable about local conditions and has accumulated a wealth of published literature on the country, which he makes available to incoming expatriates and their families.

Finally, during Unilever's long history of expatriation, its overseas operations have become well developed; expatriates do not have to venture into new frontiers. In each country there is an established Unilever community that facilitates the new arrivals' acculturation.

In the LMN Group, the rate of expatriate failure is also extremely low, around 1 percent. When it becomes evident that an expatriate is not performing well, the host company informs the person's home company. To minimize the damage to both the expatriate and the host company, the return may be accelerated. If the repatriate can be reassimilated very quickly upon return, his poor performance abroad will probably not have an adverse impact upon his subsequent career. According to one manager, "If a person fails in one culture, he is definitely given a second chance. If he fails twice, however, then you begin to think there is something wrong with him."

One of LMN's managers proffered several reasons for the low rate of expatriate failure.

One, the company's long history of expatriation works in its favor. Like Unilever, LMN has well-developed communities of expatriates in most countries, complete with schools. These communities provide strong support and assistance to new arrivals to facilitate adaptation.

Two, the company allows an initial settling-in period in the new cultural environment, making allowances for substandard performance during this time. This settling-in period, however, is not nearly as long as the three-year span in most Japanese MNCs (Tung 1984a). A primary reason for the shorter adjustment period is that LMN positions are generally specialized functions, as compared to generalist positions in Japanese multinationals. Since a specialist performs a select function abroad, he should be operational within six months after arrival, unless he is new to the function to be performed. Such a situation rarely arises because LMN's policy is to add geography to expertise, that is, to broaden the international perspective of people who are engaged in specialist functions.

A third reason for success, according to one manager, is that LMN's "culture is kind." Like Unilever, LMN does not like to view expatriate assignments as a "win-lose/succeed-fail" dichotomy. Whenever possible, the company that initiated the transfer expedites the return since the exact duration of an assignment is not specified at the time of expatriation. If a person performs extremely well in a foreign environment, however, the company may request that the home company extend his tenure abroad.

Fourth, given the stature of the LMN Group in Europe and, indeed, worldwide, the company can attract highly qualified people. Every year, from 3,000 to 4,000 university graduates apply for positions with the two parent organizations. Of these applicants, only the top 200 candidates are hired. Thus, LMN's expatriates come from a cadre of top people.

Fifth, the international orientation of many Europeans attracts potentially successful expatriate employees to LMN. According to one manager, "I think there is still a legacy of the empire in this part of the world. . . . In fact, almost everybody has a relative who is living in some other part of the world.'' Similar to the situation of XYZ Bank, many people join the LMN Group with the explicit desire to work overseas, even though their wishes may be stymied by work permit requirements and the high cost of expatriation. One LMN manager expressed his belief that ''we are raising too many hopes of going overseas. While I think this is part of the culture of LMN, I also think it is still a part of the European culture. . . . In any case, Europeans are used to going abroad on holidays. In recruiting, one usually looks for people who have traveled.''

Finally, the range of products that the LMN Group handles are basic to virtually all industries, and the company's jobs are challenging and exciting. ''I think LMN jobs are seen as rewarding because of their involvement. Our employees are highly motivated by this.'' At head-quarters the functions are more specialized, whereas expatriates' jobs provide a broader exposure to a wider range of activities. Furthermore, because of the diversity of the product groups and the extensiveness of the company's operations, ''one of the joys at LMN is that you can frequently move from company to company without having to change corporations.'' This environment engenders a greater spirit of dedication and loyalty among employees to corporate goals.

Changes

Vineall was asked to offer some thoughts on changes he would like to implement at Unilever. His suggestions are two-fold. He would like to have more lead time between the identification of a vacancy abroad and actual expatriation. ''Something has gone wrong or somebody has left or the local man isn't making out—they always need the man yesterday.'' If an employee were given at least one year's advance notice, he could ''adjust to the the idea of going overseas and think through it. . . . Everything about expatriation is complicated. . . . You get into—children, their living, and so on. And rightly so, but it does take a lot of advance planning.'' Similar changes were proposed by several executives in other European MNCs. Vineall would also like to use the Farnham program more extensively. Because of the short lead time, Farnham's courses may not be offered to coincide with the expatriation. Hence some expatriates go abroad without the benefit of this valuable program.

8 CONCLUSION

Having compared the human resource management programs with regard to selection and training of expatriates among a sample of U.S., European, and Japanese multinationals, and having examined the international human resource development programs at a number of European multinationals, we can now draw some conclusions. In general, it appears that the European MNCs, like their Japanese counterparts, send abroad individuals who are more adept at living and working in a foreign environment, as evidenced by the exceedingly low failure rates. Of the seventeen European MNCs interviewed, none had a failure rate exceeding 6 percent.

REASONS FOR LOWER FAILURE RATES AMONG EUROPEAN MNCs

Throughout the chapters, the interviewees offered reasons for the lower failure rates in their companies. These are now summarized and discussed.

International Orientation

Virtually all of the European executives interviewed considered their employees' global orientation to be a primary reason for their success in expatriation. This international perspective accounts for the relative ease with which many European expatriates adapt to new cultural settings. When failures occur, many can be attributed to health problems brought on by the foreign climatic conditions rather than by maladjustment to the cultures themselves.

This European spirit of internationalism can be ascribed to several factors. First, there is the smaller size of the domestic markets. Fully one-third of the United Kingdom's GNP is exported, for instance. As the British say, "We must export or die." In order to grow, European companies must expand their overseas markets. Sandoz, a large Swiss chemical manufacturer, generates 95 percent of its sales from abroad. This export mentality and heavy dependence on the international market stand in stark contrast to the situation in the United States, where multinationals typically derive a sizable portion of their sales and revenue from domestic operations.

Second, due to the relative smallness of European nations and their close physical proximity, most Europeans are naturally exposed to foreign people and cultures. Several executives noted that this is true even of the United Kingdom. Although separated from continental Europe by the English Channel, approximately 60 percent of its people have traveled abroad. In contrast, the executives observed that Americans do not need to vacation abroad to experience a change in scenery and climate. The United States, being a vast country, offers such variety within its own borders.

Third, certain traditions and economic conditions in Europe have long encouraged interaction abroad, and even emigration. A number of British executives noted that since World War II, the center of Western economic and military power has shifted westward across the Atlantic. This "humbling or sobering experience" forced most Britons to make a more pragmatic assessment of their nation's limitations and hence adopt a "more realistic attitude overseas." In countries like Switzerland and Italy, where there is a history of emigration to improve one's fortunes, people have a more positive attitude toward foreign lands. Switzerland's tradition of ultimogeniture, for instance, compels the elder children to leave home and make a living elsewhere. In general, there is a certain resilience among the Swiss that may be a carryover from their army training. In the words of one executive, "The Swiss make the assumption that if a person has a determination and the will to survive, that's the way to get along." Armed with this attitude, they do not expect too much abroad. The same can be said of Italians, particularly those from the farming communities in the south, which have a strong tradition of overseas emigration. According to an Italian executive, many view an assignment abroad, especially to an advanced nation, as an "enrichment." Conversely, the military and economic strength of the United States have made Americans too complacent about their culture, in the view of several executives interviewed. This self-satisfaction may often be interpreted as arrogance and thus arouse hostility and resentment among non-Americans. In short, many Europeans still view the "ugly American" syndrome as alive and thriving, particularly in the less-developed countries.

Fourth, there is the legacy of the empire. In general, European MNCs have a longer history of overseas operations. In fact, many companies included in this study established their overseas operations during the height of European imperalism. In the words of a British executive, "I suppose there is still a legacy of the Empire on this side. It is a part of British culture to travel and work overseas. There is nothing unusual for many members of one's family to have been abroad or to know many people who have worked abroad." This theme was echoed by the Germans, Italians, and Swiss.

The spirit of internationalism has affected the human resource management of European MNCs in several ways. Companies and employees alike place great value on international experience and overseas assignments. In most of the companies studied, international experience is considered an important requisite for promotion to top management. To quote Hurst of NatWest Bank, "It is known throughout the company that once a person is selected for an overseas assignment, 99 percent of the time it is a promotion." Positions abroad are often viewed as exciting and challenging because a substantial portion of the company's revenues is derived overseas. As one executive of a large Swiss multinational explained, "It doesn't mean that the jobs [in corporate headquarters] are unimportant, but it puts a somewhat different tenor on where the important jobs are." This sentiment is very different from that prevalent in many U.S. multinationals, where employees avoid international assignments because of their concerns with repatriation and reabsorption into the corporate organizational hierarchy. This attitude may be changing, however. A 1983 survey of 125 executives by Kenny, Kindler and Hunt, a recruiting firm in New York City, found that 37 percent indicated willingness to accept an overseas assignment, compared with 10 percent in 1973 (Lubin, 1983).

A second way in which the spirit of internationalism has affected human resource management practices in European firms is in the recruitment of candidates for managerial positions. In addition to people with technical competence, many European companies seek "well-traveled younggraduates" as candidates for their management trainee programs. In the case of a large British bank, the new recruits are "the children of the diplomatic corps, banks, or those who have done the traveling on their own."

A third implication of the international orientation is the heterogeneous, or multinational, composition of European firms' management teams to ensure an international perspective in all aspects of the companies' operations. Some transnational corporations, for instance, use a system of cross-country rotation of management personnel. Under this system, employees join at a local operating company, but they must have two to three years' experience in another overseas operating company before being promoted to the managerial level. Furthermore, each management team normally includes one member who is a foreign national on assignment from an overseas sister affiliate.

Finally, the greater international orientation of Europeans makes spouses typically more receptive to foreign ways of life. This receptivity may be diluted by other factors, however, such as working wives who are reluctant to give up their jobs. In the words of an executive of a British petroleum company, "The hangover from colonial days . . . the expectation of the loyal wife trotting off, following her husband and coping, is in fact going."

History of Overseas Operations

Many European MNCs expanded overseas during the heyday of European imperialism, and some British and Swiss companies trace their origins to several centuries ago. This long history of overseas operations has facilitated international human resource management in two important ways. One, the companies have accumulated a wealth of experience in dealing with foreign nationals. Many firms have resident experts who can provide valuable information and advice, whether on a formal or an informal basis, to the younger generation of expatriates. Two, the foreign operations of these MNCs are generally well established. Hence, in most cases, the expatriate moves into a developed operation abroad where everything is already in place. This facilitates his adaptation to the local environment.

In comparison, U.S. multinationals have a much shorter history of overseas operations. Thus, American expatriates do not have access to the wealth of information and resources generally available to their European counterparts.

Language Capability

While foreign language skills may not be specifically cited as an important criterion in the selection of personnel for overseas assignments, there is often an implicit assumption that "all normal people can speak four or five languages," to quote a Swiss executive. Certainly not all Europeans have facility in four or five languages, but many are bilingual or multilingual. The close physical proximity of their countries exposes them to many languages, and the importance of the international market encourages them to gain proficiency in at least some of them.

Most Americans, in contrast, are monolingual. Knowledge of a foreign language may not always guarantee effective performance abroad, but it does facilitate adaptation by enabling the expatriate to develop a comfortable rapport with coworkers, customers, and other members of the local community. In addition, knowledge of the host nation's language enables the person to gain insight into its culture. Consequently, unfamiliarity with the host-country language can be a major handicap to successful performance abroad.

Long-Term Orientation in Overall Planning and Performance Evaluation

European multinationals, like their Japanese counterparts, generally possess a long-term orientation in their management of human resources. This is exhibited in several ways. First, the rate of turnover among managerial personnel is very low or nonexistent. Mid-career changes are rare since most companies espouse a policy of promotion from within. This "cradle-to-grave" philosophy implies certain obligations and responsibilities for both the employer and the employee, similar to those found in Japanese firms (Tung 1984a). For their part, European employers are relatively tolerant of circumstances that may temporarily diminish a person's job performance, particularly during the initial period of assignment abroad. Some of the companies interviewed allowed an adjustment period of up to one year. Even in cases where the expatriate has difficulty in operating abroad, companies seldom dismiss him as a failure. In the words of one British executive "We try not to see it as a win-lose/succeed-fail dichotomy." Rather, a more suitable posting for the individual will be sought. An executive of a transnational corporation explained, "Our company culture is kind. We try to find something to suit the man. One asks, 'What is he good at?' " In return, the employees demonstrate a greater commitment to organizational goals. This loyalty and dedication, combined with the importance attached to overseas assignments, restricted job mobility, and overall qualification of the candidates (the latter two factors will be discussed subsequently), lead most European expatriates to work harder to make the foreign assignment a success.

A second result of this long-term orientation among European multi-nationals is their greater willingness to invest substantial sums of money in career development programs. This allows for more comprehensive training for expatriates, which in turn enhances their success abroad.

A third manifestation of the long-term orientation is the extended duration of overseas assignments. Except for postings made strictly for career development, expatriate assignments in European MNCs last an average of five years or more. Often expatriates are willing to make long-term commitments to highly desirable positions located abroad rather than at domestic headquarters. Moreover, the longer duration of overseas assignments allows them more time to adjust to the new work situation and also provides incentive for them to absorb some of the local culture. Any concerns the expatriates may have about repatriation are allayed by the companies' comprehensive support systems. Until the 1960s and 1970s many European MNCs employed career expatriates. The trend toward localization, however, has led to the phasing out of such positions in many companies. (Several Swiss MNCs interviewed for this study still have career expatriates.)

A fourth implication of the long-term orientation among European multinationals is the tendency to place the same, if not more, emphasis on a person's potential as on his actual performance in assessing his overall contribution to the organization. Given the practice of life time employ-ment among most managerial personnel, the companies actually benefit from taking this approach.

In contrast to European and Japanese multinationals, U.S. multina-tionals, indeed U.S. firms in general, are characterized by a short-term orientation in planning and assessment of performance. This orientation engenders several problems. One, it may prompt managers to take actions that boost short-term profit, but that are inconsistent with the goals of long-term growth and development of market share. Two, it may explain why most U.S. multinationals do not provide formal training to prepare their expatriates for cross-cultural encounters. Companies are reluctant to invest large sums of money in training employees who may then leave for better jobs elsewhere. Given the high mobility in the U.S. work force this is not an unsubstantiated fear. Three, it may actually contribute to poor performance by increasing expatriates' anxieties. Because of concerns with repatriation, many U.S. expatriates are reluctant to serve for extended periods of time abroad. Therefore, most U.S. companies send their employees overseas for less than three years. This, however, places the expatriates under tremendous pressure to perform immediately, which is not conducive to success abroad. Research (Harrari and Zeira 1978) has shown that relieving expatriates of administrative responsibilities in the initial six months abroad facilitates their adjustment to the foreign country, thus resulting in higher levels of performance.

Training for Cross-cultural Encounters

Given the low turnover rate among management personnel, European companies, like their Japanese counterparts, are willing to invest large sums of money to develop their employees' managerial skills. Since they consider international experience an important part of career development, most companies provide in- or out-of-house programs to prepare candidates for assignments to locations outside of West Europe, North America, and Australia. While these programs differ in content and emphasis, they often include language training, cross-cultural training, and discussions with returned expatriates.

Many Europeans have studied a second or third language in school. Consequently, Bertlitz-type refresher courses are often sufficient. A few of the MNCs interviewed offered training in exotic languages such as Japanese, Chinese, or Arabic. The latter programs are, of course, more extended.

For cross-cultural training, many of the European MNCs studied use the Center for International Briefing, Farnham Castle (U.K.). It offers two types of residential programs: a four-day regional program and a week-long cultural awareness workshop. Given the center's ambience as an eleventh-century castle and the fact that the participants must remain on the castle grounds for the duration of the program, the training experience is "not so much an intellectual exercise as it is an emotional one," as Patrick Lloyd explained. This is, of course, the crux of successful adaptation to a new cultural environment. The programs are generally attended by both husband and wife. As described by a British executive, the principal benefit of the regional program is not so much comprehensive understanding of another country, since this is clearly impossible within the context of four days. Rather, it can "dent people's overconfidence that they understand by saying that is different, and you are not going to change it because it will go on being different since it has been different for a long time. So the best thing is to accept the difference.'' Other frequently used cross-cultural training facilities include the Tropen Institute (Amsterdam, Netherlands) and the Carl-Duisberg Center and Evangelische Akademie (Bad Boll, West Germany). The programs they offer are similar to those at Farnham.

Most European MNCs provide ample opportunity for outgoing families to discuss their overseas assignments with expatriates who have returned. Those companies with long histories of overseas operations usually have a fairly large contingent of resident experts, located either in corporate headquarters or abroad, who can brief expatriates and their spouses about the overseas situation. Additional contact with previous expatriates is also available. In the United Kingdom, for instance, a private, nonprofit organization called the Women's Corona Society sponsors a ''Living Overseas'' program for wives of expatriates. The program consists of lectures and discussions of problems encountered most often by families living abroad.

In comparison, U.S. multinationals generally do not provide rigorous programs to prepare their expatriates for cross-cultural encounters for two primary reasons. One, the relatively rapid rate of employee turnover may render the provision of such programs too costly. Two, these companies place more emphasis on the domestic market than on the international arena.

Support Systems in Corporate Headquarters

In general, the European multinationals, like their Japanese counterparts, have designed comprehensive support systems to help allay expatriate concerns about problems of repatriation. One such system is ''parenting,'' or ''mentoring,'' whereby an expatriate is paired to a superior in corporate headquarters who takes on the role of sponsor. The sponsor, usually a member of senior management, apprises the expatriate regularly about the situation at home and is responsible for finding a position for the expatriate upon his return. Since the turnover rate at the senior management level in most European firms is virtually zero, the expatriate can feel secure that the sponsor will be there when he returns. In the words of a British petroleum executive, even though the sponsor may have taken a new position elsewhere in the company, ''the personal link is the vital thing, not the link by way of the role the general manager [played at the time] the expatriate went out.''

Where there is no sponsor-expatriate pairing on a one-on-one basis, most companies have departments or divisions charged with overseeing the career paths of expatriates. The expatriate is required to talk to personnel from these departments during his home leave, which is usually once a year. In addition, some companies have a senior manager in their overseas subsidiaries who has what one executive termed "a part-time responsibility as a career manager or godfather." Expatriate communities in the various foreign countries also reinforce the support mechanisms provided by corporate headquarters. Given their years of operations, the foreign subsidiaries are generally well established and have relatively large expatriate communities. Thus, the new arrivals are "fairly well looked after."

Unfortunately, most U.S. multinationals do not provide adequate support mechanisms to allay expatriate concerns about possible problems of repatriation.

Qualification of Candidates

European MNCs tend to send abroad their best people. In the words of a British executive, "We won't have any hope of acceptance in the host country unless [the expatriate] is visibly and perceptibly better than the local people." This theme was echoed by numerous executives from the United Kingdom, Italy, and Switzerland. This is quite different from the U.S. situation, where it is not uncommon for the company to send abroad people "who are a bit of a nuisance or embarrassment to the company."

Restricted Job Mobility

Due to the smaller size of domestic markets in Europe, each country can generally support a limited number of firms in a given industry, thus limiting job mobility. In Italy, for instance, career opportunities for chemical engineers are restricted to positions at Montedison, a private entity, or at ENI, the public sector. Since the benefits associated with one are superior to the other, the choice is narrowed even further.

This problem may be compounded by the slower rate of economic growth in many European countries during recent years, which has resulted in massive layoffs. In one British petroleum firm, for instance, the redundancy rate reached 45 percent in 1983. The company's executive noted that "under these circumstances, people are less ready to complain." As a result of restricted job mobility, employees are generally more dedicated to organizational goals.

It is clear that numerous factors have contributed to the low rate of failure in expatriate assignments among European MNCs. However, this is not to suggest that these corporations do not encounter problems in the area of international human resource management. Two of the most pressing issues are dual-career families and the increasing reluctance of parents to leave their children in boarding schools. These problems are not dissimilar to ones encountered in the United States, however, and multinationals on both sides of the Atlantic should strive to find solutions to them.

IMPLICATIONS FOR U.S. MNCS

Several common denominators to successful performance emerge from the foregoing analysis. Like their Japanese counterparts, European multinationals benefit from placing a heavy emphasis on the international market and adopting a long-term orientation with regard to international human resource management planning. These factors lead to a greater willingness to (1) sponsor rigorous programs preparing expatriates for cross-cultural encounters, (2) provide comprehensive support systems facilitating adaptation abroad, and (3) allay concerns about repatriation problems. In addition, European MNCs enjoy the advantage of having been abroad longer, thus providing them with greater experience and a larger pool of in-house talent and resources. To compensate for their relatively recent entry into the international economic arena, the Japanese MNCs have acquired an advantage by embarking on meticulous programs to prepare their expatriates for the challenges of living and working abroad (Tung 1984a). U.S. multinationals, on the other hand, possess neither the inherent advantage of the Europeans nor the acquired advantage of the Japanese.

Can this situation among U.S. multinationals be rectified? If so, how? At least three primary implications for U.S. firms can be drawn from the foregoing analysis.

First, U.S. multinationals should develop a longer term orientation with regard to expatriate assignments, overall planning, and performance assessment. Their short-term stratgegies are incompatible with the evolving trend toward the globalization of industries, which necessitates a more international perspective among top management. Such a perspective can be engendered through one or two fairly lengthy tours of duty abroad. Short stints abroad are not conducive to high performance because they give the expatriate insufficient time to adjust to the new job and culture. Particularly with overseas assignments undertaken primarily for career-development purposes, it is important to allow an adequate adjustment period since dismal performance abroad erodes the expatriates' self-confidence, thus diminishing their attractiveness for top management positions.

To allay expatriate concerns that prolonged absence from corporate headquarters may negatively affect their opportunities for promotion, U.S. companies should implement support mechanisms similar to those already instituted by European and Japanese MNCs. While one-on-one mentoring may not be possible given the more rapid turnover of American management personnel, the institution of separate departments or divisions whose sole function is to oversee the career paths of expatriates should be feasible.

A longer term orientation may also engender greater commitment and loyalty among employees and increased willingness to undergo temporary inconveniences in order to advance the company's overall goals. Longer durations of assignment will provide an incentive for expatriates to absorb some of the customs and perhaps learn the language of their assigned countries. Furthermore, greater employee loyalty may lower the incidence of turnover, which should increase companies' willingness to invest in training programs.

A second implication of this study is that U.S. multinationals, and American society in general, must develop a more international orientation. Without a fundamental change of attitude in this regard, the international market will continue to be relegated a secondary role in corporate planning. Under these circumstances, it is unrealistic to expect that companies will devote sufficient attention to the area of international human resource management. As the technological gap continues to narrow between the United States, Europe, and Japan, U.S. multinationals can no longer rely solely on technology to gain a competitive edge in international markets. The successful operation of a multinational is increasingly contingent upon the availability of additional resources, such as capital, know-how, and human power. It is argued that human power is a key ingredient in the efficient operation of a multinational because other resources are not as effectively and efficiently allocated to subsidiaries by corporate headquarters in the absence of a highly developed pool of managerial talent possessing international orientation. The international competitiveness of U.S. multinationals hinges on the ingenuity of its workers, and more importantly, those sent overseas as representatives of corporate headquarters. There are encouraging signs that the United States has finally awakened to this situation, evidenced by the burgeoning interest in international business and cross-cultural programs at academic institutions, particularly at the university level. This is just a beginning, however; much more needs to be done.

A third implication of this study is that U.S. multinationals must provide more comprehensive training programs to prepare their expatriates for cross-cultural encounters. Other studies have shown that technical competence alone is a necessary but insufficient condition for successful operations abroad. American corporations may be reluctant to invest in expensive, rigorous programs, such as those found in the Japanese MNCs, because workers may not remain in their employ long enough to justify the output. However, programs along the lines of those offered by the Center for International Briefing, Farnham Castle should certainly be feasible. It is clearly impossible to prepare expatriates for all the contingencies of living and working abroad within the course of a one-week program. An executive with a large European transnational corporation suggests, however, that a Farnham-type program can ''at least dent people's overconfidence'' in the superiority of their own ways of thinking and operating. Such programs emphasize that cultural differences have existed for centuries.

By examining and then implementing the aforementioned changes, the dismal record of U.S. expatriate performance can begin to improve. As Patrick Lloyd of Farnham Castle succinctly put it, ''Expatriate failure is very costly. Not only are we referring to the hundreds of thousands of pounds it costs to send the person overseas, but failure damages the reputation of the company. In the case of an expatriate's inability to adjust to a different culture, people don't say: 'He is a funny person that you sent here.' They will say: 'Why did that company send that person here?' Companies have to assess whether the person can deliver that professional capability overseas.'' With the increasing globalization of industry, U.S. multinationals can no longer afford a nonchalant attitude toward the development and management of international human resources, a pivotal force in successful global competition.

APPENDIX:
Questionnaire for U.S. Sample

> When completing the following items contained in this questionnaire, please note the following:
>
> (1) For purposes of the study, the word "affiliate" includes branches, subsidiaries, joint ventures and minority investments.
>
> (2) Some of the information requested pertain to regions of the world in which your company may not have foreign operations. Please omit those items or sections. Only answer those items or sections that are relevant to the regions of your company's operations abroad.
>
> (3) If the information requested on relevant regions is not available, please provide some approximate estimates.

1. Your affiliate operations are located in:

        (   )   Western Europe

        (   )   Canada

        (   )   Middle and Near East

        (   )   Eastern Europe

        (   )   Latin and South America

        (   )   Far East

        (   )   Africa

The questions in this section are aimed at obtaining information regarding positions of different management levels in your affiliate operation(s) abroad and how they are staffed. For this purpose, the following terms mean:

(1) "Parent Country Nationals":   These refer to personnel who are U.S. citizens.

(2) "Host Country Nationals":   These refer to personnel who are citizens of the country of foreign operation.

(3) "Third Country Nationals":   These refer to personnel who are neither citizens of the U.S. nor country in which the foreign operation is located.

PART I

Please indicate your response by a (✓). Limit your answers only to those regions that are relevant to your company's operations abroad.

WESTERN EUROPE	CANADA
a. Senior management positions in this region are primarily staffed by:	a. Senior management positions in this region are primarily staffed by:
( ) parent country nationals	( ) parent country nationals
( ) host country nationals	( ) host country nationals
( ) third country nationals	( ) third country nationals
b. Middle management positions in this region are primarily staffed by:	b. Middle management positions in this region are primarily staffed by:
( ) parent country nationals	( ) parent country nationals
( ) host country nationals	( ) host country nationals
( ) third country nationals	( ) third country nationals
c. Lower level management positions in this region are primarily staffed by:	c. Lower level management positions in this region are primarily staffed by:
( ) parent country nationals	( ) parent country nationals
( ) host country nationals	( ) host country nationals
( ) third country nationals	( ) third country nationals

MIDDLE AND NEAR EAST	EASTERN EUROPE
a. Senior management positions in this region are primarily staffed by: ( ) parent country nationals ( ) host country nationals ( ) third country nationals	a. senior management positions in this region are primarily staffed by: ( ) parent country nationals ( ) host country nationals ( ) third country nationals
b. Middle management positions in this region are primarily staffed by: ( ) parent country nationals ( ) host country nationals ( ) third country nationals	b. Middle management positions in this region are primarily staffed by: ( ) parent country nationals ( ) host country nationals ( ) third country nationals
c. Lower level management positions in this region are primarily staffed by: ( ) parent country nationals ( ) host country nationals ( ) third country nationals	c. Lower level management positions in this region are are primarily staffed by: ( ) parent country nationals ( ) host country nationals ( ) third country nationals

LATIN AND SOUTH AMERICA	FAR EAST
a. Senior management positions in this region are primarily staffed by:	a. senior management positions in this region are primarily staffed by:
( ) parent country nationals	( ) parent country nationals
( ) host country nationals	( ) host country nationals
( ) third country nationals	( ) third country nationals
b. Middle management positions in this region are primarily staffed by:	b. Middle management positions in this region are primarily staffed by:
( ) parent country nationals	( ) parent country nationals
( ) host country nationals	( ) host country nationals
( ) third country nationals	( ) third country nationals
c. Lower level management positions in this region are primarily staffed by:	c. Lower level management positions in this region are are primarily staffed by:
( ) parent country nationals	( ) parent country nationals
( ) host country nationals	( ) host country nationals
( ) third country nationals	( ) third country nationals

AFRICA

a. Senior management positions
    in this region are primarily
    staffed by:

    (   )   parent country nationals

    (   )   host country nationals

    (   )   third country nationals

b. Middle management positions
    in this region are primarily
    staffed by:

    (   )   parent country nationals

    (   )   host country nationals

    (   )   third country nationals

c. Lower level management
    positions in this region are
    primarily staffed by:

    (   )   parent country nationals

    (   )   host country nationals

    (   )   third country nationals

PART II

A.   Check one or more of the applicable reasons below for staffing overseas
     operations with parent country nationals (i.e. personnel who are U.S.
     citizens):

( )   a.   The foreign enterprise is just being established (start-up
           phase).

( )   b.   The parent firm wishes to develop an internationally
           oriented management for the headquarters (foreign
           assignments are seen essentially as management
           development).

( )   c.   No adequate management is available from other countries.

( )   d.   The parent firm has surplus managerial personnel toward
           whom it feels responsible.

( )   e.   Virtually no autonomy is possible for the foreign
           enterprise because it is integrated so closely with
           operations elsewhere.

( )   f.   The foreign enterprise is seen as short-lived.

( )   g.   The host society is multiracial or multireligious, and a
           local manager of either racial origin or religion would
           make the enterprise potentially vulnerable or lead to an
           economic boycott.

( )   h.   There is a compelling need to maintain a foreign image.

( )   i.   It is felt desirable to avoid involving particular local
           nationals or families (former distributors or agents) in
           management, and the use of other local nationals would
           create dangerous animosities.

( )   j.   Local nationals are not mobile and resist assignment
           elsewhere.

( )   k.   A parent country national is simply the best man for the
           job, all things considered.

( )   l.   Control is weak, particularly in cases where local
           nationals are highly nationalistic (patriotic) and more
           responsive to government pressures than would an
           expatriate.

( )   m.   Technical expertise.

( )   n.   Many times our clients request U.S. nationals.

( )   o.   Other (specify):_____

B. Check one or more of the applicable reasons below for staffing overseas operations with third country nationals (i.e., personnel who are neither citizens of the U.S. nor of the country of foreign operations):

( ) a. Reduced costs.

( ) b. Technical expertise.

( ) c. The host society is multiracial or multireligious, and a local manager of either racial origin or religion would make the enterprise politically vulnerable or lead to an economic boycott.

( ) d. It is felt desirable to avoid involving particular local nationals or families (former distributors or agents) in management, and the use of other local nationals would create dangerous animosities.

( ) e. U.S. personnel are generally less interested in overseas assignments, particularly in out-of-the-way locations.

( ) f. A third country national is simply the best man for the job, all things considered.

( ) g. No adequate management is available from other sources.

( ) h. Language skills that parent country nationals do not possess.

( ) i. Other (specify):_____

C. Check one or more of the applicable reasons below for staffing overseas operations with host country nationals (i.e. personnel who are citizens of the country of foreign operation):

( ) a. Reduced costs.

( ) b. Denial of entry of aliens.

( ) c. Denial of work permit to aliens.

( ) d. Knowledge of language.

( ) e. Greater familiarity with the local culture.

( ) f. Good public relations

( ) g. A host country national is simply the best man for the job, all things considered.

( ) h. No adequate management is available from other sources.

( ) i. Other (specify):_____

PART III

> In selecting "parent country nationals" to fill overseas assignments, you
> may base your selection decision on a set of criteria. You may or may not use
> the same set of criteria for selecting people to fill overseas managerial
> positions. For purposes of this study, we will classify overseas managerial
> assignments according to four general categories. These are:
>
> (1) Chief Executive Officer: whose responsibility is to oversee and
>   direct the entire foreign operation.
>
> (2) Functional Head: whose job is to establish functional
>   departments is a foreign subsidiary.
>
> (3) Trouble-Shooter: whose function is to analyze and solve
>   specific operational problems.
>
> (4) Operative: rank-and-file members.

For each of the four categories, please identify the criteria that you may use
for selecting people by checking the appropriate boxes.

Criteria	Chief Executive Officer			Functional Head			Trouble Shooter			Operative		
	Criterion Not Used	Use, Not Important	Use, Very Important	Criterion Not Used	Use, Not Important	Use, Very Important	Criterion Not Used	Use, Not Important	Use, Very Important	Criterion Not Used	Use, Not Important	Use, Very Important
Experience in company												
Technical knowledge of business												
Knowledge of language of host country												
Overall experience and education of candidate												
Managerial talent												
Interest in overseas work												
Initiative, creativity												
Independence												
Previous overseas experience												
Respect of laws and people of host country												
Sex/gender												
Age												
Stability of marital relations												
Spouse and family's adaptability												
Adaptability, flexibility in new environmental surroundings												
Maturity, emotional stability												
Communication												
Same criteria as other comparable jobs at home												
Other (specify):												

PART IV

Please identify the steps that you may go through in selecting a candidate for foreign assignment.

a. Are tests administered to determine the candidates technical competence?

        Yes (   )   No (   )

b. Are tests administered to determine the candidate's relational abilities i.e., ability to empathize with different cultural values and norms?

        Yes (   )   No (   )

If yes, briefly describe the nature of the tests used to determine the candidate's relational abilities.

_____

_____

_____

_____

_____

c. For management positions, are interviews conducted with the candidate? Please check one.

        Yes, with both (   )   Yes, with (   )   No (   )
        candidate and   candidate
        and spouse   only

d. For technical positions, are interviews conducted with the candidate? Please check one.

        Yes, with both (   )   Yes, with (   )   No (   )
        candidate and   candidate
        and spouse   only

PART V

Every year, some managers may have to be recalled to their home country or their employment terminated because of their inability to function effectively in a foreign environment. Below are a list of possible reasons for such failures.

A.   In your opinion, how often are such failures (in your company and other companies you are familiar with) attributable to each of the reasons given below? Please indicate your response by placing a (✓) in the appropriate columns.

Reasons for failures	This reason does not apply	To a very little extent	To a little extent	To some extent	To a great extent	To a very great extent
Inability of the manager to cope with the larger responsibilities posed by the overseas work.						
Lack of motivation to work overseas.						
Manager's personality or emotional maturity.						
Manager's lack of technical competence for the job assignment.						
The manager's inability to adapt to a different physical or cultural environment.						
The inability of the manager's spouse to adjust to a different cultural or physical environment.						
Other family-related problems.						
Other (specify):						

B.   What percentage of overseas personnel have to be recalled to their home
     country or dismissed because of inability to function effectively in a
     foreign assignment? Please check one.

          (   )   Between 0 - 5%

          (   )   Between 6 - 10%

          (   )   Between 11 - 15%

          (   )   Between 16 - 19%

          (   )   Between 20 - 39%

          (   )   Between 40 - 59%

          (   )   Between 60 - 80%

          (   )   Over 80%

C.   In your organization, after a candidate from corporate headquarters has
     been selected for a foreign assignment, does he/she have to undergo a
     special formalized training program to prepare for the overseas work?

               Yes (   )   No   (   )

     If "no," what are the reasons for omitting formal training prior to
     overseas assignment? Please check one or more of the following reasons:

          (   )   Temporary nature of many assignments.

          (   )   Lack of time because of the immediacy of the need for the
                     employee overseas.

          (   )   Trend toward employment of local nationals.

          (   )   Doubt effectiveness of existing training programs.

PART VI

Companies may sponsor formal training programs to prepare their candidates for overseas assignments. Please indicate by a (✓) the type of training program that your organization has for candidates who would be taking up overseas managerial positions in each of the four categories.

(1)	Chief Executive Officer:	whose responsibility is to oversee and direct the entire foreign operation.
(2)	Functional Head:	whose job is to establish functional departments is a foreign subsidiary.
(3)	Trouble-Shooter:	whose function is to analyze and solve specific operational problems.
(4)	Operative:	rank-and-file members.

Type of Training Program	Chief Executive Officer	Functional Head	Trouble Shooter	Operative
Language Training				
Cultural Orientation--information about the cultural institutions, value systems of host country				
Environmental Briefing--information about the geography, climate, housing, schools, etc.				
Cultural Assimilator--brief episodes describing inter-cultural encounters				
Sensitivity Training--to develop attitudinal flexibility				
Field Experience--wherein trainees are actually sent to the country of assignment or a "micro culture" nearby, where they could undergo some of the emotional stress that they would expect in living and working with people from a different sub-culture/culture.				
Other (specify):				

B.   Is there any evaluation of the effectiveness of the formal training programs currently utilized by your company? Check one:

Yes (   )   No (   )   Don't know (   )

If "yes," please indicate the procedures used to evaluate the effectiveness of such training programs.

(   )   Trainee's subjective evaluation of the usefulness of training programs

(   )   Supervisor's subjective evaluation of trainee's performance after formal training.

(   )   Objective tests (e.g., aptitude tests, etc.)

(   )   Others (specify):_____

_____

_____

_____

_____

_____

_____

THANK YOU VERY MUCH FOR YOUR COOPERATION

Name of firm (optional):

_____

REFERENCES

Adams, T.E.M., and Kobayashi, N. 1969. *The World of Japanese Business*. Tokyo: Kodnsha International.

Borrmann, W.A. 1968. "The Problem of Expatriate Personnel and Their Selection in International Business." *Management International Review* 8, no. 4/5: 37–48.

Campbell, R.D. 1969. "United States Miltary Training for Cross-Cultural Interaction." Occasional paper. U.S. *Office of Naval Research*, June 4.

Deutsch, S.E. 1970. *International Education and Exchange: A Sociological Analysis*. Cleveland, Oh.: Case Western Reserve University Press.

Drucker, P. 1954. *The Practice of Management*. New York: Harper and Row.

Dymsza, W.A. 1972. *Multinational Business Strategy*. New York: McGraw-Hill.

Fiat 1983. *Annual Report*. Torino, Italy.

Fiedler, F.E., and Mitchell, T. 1971. "The Culture Assimilator: An Approach to Cross-Cultural Training." *Journal of Applied Psychology* 55, no. 2: 95–102.

Harrari, E., and Zeira, Y. 1978. "Training Expatriates for Managerial Assignments in Japan." *California Management Review* 20, no. 4: 56–62.

Harris, P.R., and Harris, D.L. 1972. "Training for Cultural Understanding." *Training and Development Journal* (May): 8–10.

Harrison, R., and Hopkins, R.L. 1967. "The Design of Cross-Cultural Training." *Journal of Applied Behavioral Science* 3, no. 4: 431–60.

Hays, R.D. 1971. "Ascribed Behavioral Determinants of Success-Failure among U.S. Expatriate Managers." *Journal of International Business Studies* 2, no. 1 (Spring): 40–46.

——— . 1974. "Expatriate Selection: Insuring Success and Avoiding Failure." *Journal of International Business Studies* 5, no. 1 (Spring): 25–37.

Henry, E.R. 1965. "What Business Can Learn from the Peace Corps Selection and Training." *Personnel* 42, no. 4 (July-August): 17–25.

Hofstede, G.H. 1984. *Culture's Consequences: International Differences in Work-Related Values*. Beverly Hills, Calif.: Sage Publicatons.

Howard, C.G. 1974. "Model for the Design of a Selection Program for Multinational Executives." *Public Personnel Management* (March-April): 138–45.

International Education Center, 1982 Brochure. Tokyo, Japan.

IIST. 1980-81 Brochure. Fujinomiya, Japan: IIST.

———— . *Practical Trade Program.* Fujinomiya, Japan: IIST.

Itabashi, N. 1978. "Adult Education: English Teaching at a Language School." In *The Teaching of English in Japan*, pp. 169–86. Tokyo: Eichosha Publishing Co.

———— . 1982. Correspondence with the author, November 16.

Ivancevich, J.M. 1969. "Selection of America Managers for Overseas Assignments." *Personnel Journal* 48, no. 3 (March): 189–93, 200.

Japan Economic News, June 24, 1982.

Japan Overseas Educational Services. 1982. *Training Program for Spouses.* Tokyo: Japan Overseas Educational Services.

Kawaji, K. 1982. "Selection of Personnel for a Long-Term Overseas Assignment." Tokyo: Mitsubishi Electric Co. Ltd.

Lublin, J.S. 1983. "Overseas Work Appeals to More U.S. Managers as a Wise Career Move." *Wall Street Journal*, July 19, p. 1.

Lynton, R.P., and Pareek, U. 1967. *Training for Development.* Chicago, Ill.: Dorsey Press.

"Management Development in the Brown Boveri Group," February 1, 1977. Baden, Switzerland.

Matsuno, S., and Stoever, W.A. 1982. "Japanese Boss, American Employees." *Wharton Magazine*, Fall, pp. 45–48.

Miller, E.L. 1972. "The Selection Decision for an International Assignment: A Study of the Decision Maker's Behavior." *Journal of International Business Studies* 3, no. 1 (Spring): 49–65.

Misrachi, C. 1985. "Politique de Gestion Du Personnel International Des "Enterprises Françaises." Paris: Inter Cultural Management Associates.

Nippon: The Land and Its People. 1983. Tokyo: Nippon Steel Corporation.

Olivetti. 1983. *Consolidated Financial Statements.* Ivrea, Italy.

Pascale, R.T., and Athos, A.G. 1981. *The Art of Japanese Management.* New York: Simon and Schuster.

Peters, T.J., and Waterman, R.H., Jr. 1982. *In Search of Excellence: Lessons From American's Best-Run Companies.* New York: Harper and Row.

"Policy of the BBC Konzern on International Personnel Transfers," February 24, 1982. Baden, Switzerland.

Rubin, I. 1967. "The Reduction of Prejudice through Laboratory Training." *Journal of Applied Behavioral Science* 3, no. 1 (January-February): 29–50.

School of International Studies. 1982. *Brochure.* Tokyo.

Seward, J. 1975. "Speaking the Japanese Business Language." *European Business* (Winter): 40–47.

Sieveking, N., Anchor, K., and Marston, R.C. 1981. "Selecting and Preparing Expatriate Employees." *Personnel Journal* (March): 197–202.

Textor, R.B., ed. 1966. *Cultural Frontiers of the Peace Corps.* Cambridge, Mass.: MIT Press.

Tung, R.L. 1981. "Selection and Training of Personnel for Overseas Assignments." *Columbia Journal of World Business* (Spring): 68–78.

_____ . 1982. "Selection and Training Procedures of U.S., European, and Japanese Multinationals." *California Management Review* 25, 1: 57–71.

_____ . 1984a. *Key to Japan's Economic Strength: Human Power*. Lexington, Mass.: Lexington Books, D.C. Heath.

_____ . 1984b. *Business Negotiations with the Japanese*. Lexington, Mass.: Lexington Books, D.C. Heath.

_____ . 1986. *Strategic Management in the United States and Japan: A Comparative Analysis*. Cambridge, Mass.: Ballinger.

Useem, J., Useem, R., and Donoghue, J. 1963. "Men in the Middle of the Third Culture." *Human Organization* 22, no. 3 (Fall): 169–179.

INDEX

ABOUT THE AUTHOR

Rosalie L. Tung (Ph.D., University of British Columbia) is professor of business administration and director of the International Business Center at the University of Wisconsin, Milwaukee. She has served on the faculties of the Wharton School, University of Pennsylvania; the University of Oregon; the University of California, Los Angeles; and the University of Manchester Institute of Science and Technology, England. She was invited as the first foreign expert to teach management at the Foreign Investment Commission (now known as the Ministry of Foreign Economic Relations and Trade), the highest agency under the Chinese State Council that approves all joint ventures and other major forms of foreign investment.

Professor Tung is the author of six books: *Management Practices in China*, in the *China—International Business Series* (Pergamon, 1980); *U.S.— China Trade Negotiations* (Pergamon, 1982); *Chinese Industrial Society after Mao* (D.C. Heath, 1982); *Business Negotiations with the Japanese* (D.C. Heath, 1984); *Key to Japan's Economic Strength: Human Power* (D.C. Heath, 1984); and *Strategic Management in the United States and Japan: A Comparative Analysis* (Ballinger 1986). She has also published widely on the subjects of international management and organizational theory in leading professional journals such as the *Columbia Journal of World Business, Journal of International Business Studies, Academy of Management Executive, California Management Review, Academy of Management Journal, Academy of Management Review, Journal of Vocational Behavior, Journal of Applied Psychology, Human Resource Management, Wharton Annual, Pacific Basin Economic Review*, and *Euro-Asia Business Review*. Her research has been cited in various national and international newspapers, including the *International Herald Tribune*, the *Wall Street Journal*, the *Christian Science Monitor, Business Week*, and *East Asian Executive Reports*.

Professor Tung is currently a member of the Board of Governors, Academy of Management. She is also a past chairperson of the International Management Division, Academy of Management and has served as a treasurer and member of the Executive Board, Academy of International Business. She is a reviewer of peer proposals for the National Science Foundation and the U.S. Department of Education and sits on the editorial board of several academic journals. Dr. Tung has lectured widely at leading universities throughout the world and is active in the internationalization efforts of business schools worldwide. She has been appointed to the Commercial Panel of Arbitrators, American Arbitration Association and is actively involved in management development and consulting activities around the world. She has been included in *Who's Who in the World, The International Who's Who of Intellectuals, The World's Who's Who of Women, Who's Who of American Women,* and elsewhere for outstanding contributions in her field.